D1565642

The Exemplary Life of Moorfield Storey

MOORFIELD
NAACP's First President
Paving the Way for Modern Day Activism

ELVIS SLAUGHTER

© 2022

ISBN: 978-1-7360506-3-7

World Press Publishing

Slaughter & Associates

P. O. Box 314

Calumet City, IL 60409

www.worldpresspublishing.org

Library of Congress Control Number: 2022937953

CONTENTS

Dedicated to Jim Storey

November 3, 2019

Dear Mr. Slaughter,

I am so pleased to receive your letter. (...) I never knew my grandfather (he died three years before I was born). I am 88 years old, but, like you, I have read a lot about him, and I admired the NAACP and am glad to hear that it is still going strong. (...)

Thank you for your interest in my grandfather and for writing me. I thank you personally for your very nice letter. It is very welcoming, and I appreciate your interest in my grandfather.

Sincerely,

Jim Storey

ACKNOWLEDGMENT

HAVE HAD THE opportunity to connect with people who have made measurable and true impacts through my lifetime membership with the NAACP. Their sense of purpose and dedication to bettering the lives of others were the qualities that spurred my admiration of the NAACP's late prominent members, Nola Bright and Julian Bond.

Nola was like my godmother, helping raise me when I lived on the westside of Chicago, including feeding and clothing me. Her compassionate and loving heart gave me the gift of openness to see, learn, and experience new things and be a better servant of the cause and the world at large. She marched with Dr. Martin Luther King, Jessie Jackson, and others. When she took me under her wing and asked me to be the first Vice President of the Chicago Westside NAACP Branch, I learned courage and selflessness.

Julian Bond understood the power of connection, relationships, and engaging with the world openly. This was evident in his sincere smile and incredible strength as a prominent civil rights activist and NAACP chairman. Those traits were clear when we met. His advice and wisdom gave me the adrenaline and inspiration to stand taller for righteousness. In 1988, he became chair of the NAACP board of directors, a job he referred to as "the most powerful job a black man can have in America."

His sentiment shows the incredible power our NAACP leaders wield locally and nationally, including the chairman, board of directors, president, regional directors, state presidents, and unit presidents; all are elected or appointed officials and staff. These individuals hold some of the most powerful and, at times, rewarding positions in America.

I also want to acknowledge those who affected change by establishing the NAACP in 1909. Those sixty white, black, Jewish, and other individuals, who believed change would bring a better way to live, are the reason this organization stands tall today.

INTRODUCTION

B ORN ON MARCH 19, 1845, in Roxbury, Massachusetts (now part of Boston), Moorfield Storey first attended Boston Latin School and later, in 1862, Harvard. He graduated as the sixth scholar in the class. His father was Charles William Storey, also a graduate of Harvard. Charles Storey's well-known friends included James Russell Lowell, Dr. Oliver Wendell Holmes, and Judge Hoar. He was described by those who knew him as a popular, agreeable person. Storey's mother was a strong-willed, energetic, and resolute woman who possessed a strong New England conscience.

Many who were close to Storey agreed that he combined the qualities of his parents to a significant degree. He inherited his mother's adherence to conscience, and from his father, he inherited both geniality and charm.

While in Harvard Law School, Storey was invited to be the private secretary to Senator Charles Sumner, a position he occupied in Washington for a year. It was while serving Sumner that the impeachment of Andrew Johnson took place. Interestingly, Storey was in the Senate gallery when the popular vote was taken. The results hung in the balance until they reached the name of Ross.

It is not hard to discern some factors that influenced his life while in Washington. The political and public affairs Storey was exposed to gave him a robust view of public affairs. More importantly, he was influenced remarkably by Sumner's strong personality. Storey had ample opportunity to observe Sumner's engagement in the battle for human rights.

Shortly after returning to Boston, Storey began his ascent of the legal ladder when he accepted the post of Assistant District Attorney for Suffolk County. Because of his excellent performance, he was invited to become a junior partner of Brooks and Ball. Later, he formed the firm Storey, Thorndike & Hoar with his classmate, John L. Thorndike.[1]

While working in the new law firm, Storey was mainly in charge of the court work and became the chief adviser of several clients drawn to him. In 1894, he was made the president of the American Bar Association; later, he held similar positions in Boston's Bar Association and the Massachusetts Bar Association. His numerous literary works prove his versatility[2] and include *Life of Charles Sumner* and *Problems of Today*. The latter was delivered at the Godkin Foundation (Harvard) and the Storrs Lectures (Yale); it was later published under the title *Reforms of Legal Procedure*.

Other literary works include *Politics as a Duty and as a Career* (1899); *The Negro Question* (1918); *The Democratic Party and Philippines Independence* (1915); and *Marked Severities*, which he wrote to reveal to Americans how the U.S. executed the war in the Philippines. His most recent publication was the book he co-authored with Marcial Lichauco, entitled, *The Conquest of the Philippine Islands by the United States*. Mr. Lichauco was, at the time, the only Filipino to graduate from Harvard College.

His Bar colleagues fondly remembered him as a conversationalist of untold charm, a genial and kind friend, a sympathetic listener, and a host of abounding hospitality. Storey loved dancing during his younger days, and most of his days while in Washington were spent fully engaged. On October 24, 1929, as happens to every mortal, Storey died. He passed quietly at his residence in Lincoln after living what was described as an honored life in his community and at the Bar.[1]

Unstintingly, Storey gave his time and talent to numerous causes while serving in different capacities – as president of the Anti-Imperialist League, the Massachusetts Reform Club, the Indian Rights Association, the Massachusetts Civil Service Reform Association, the National Association for the Advancement of Colored People, and the Boston Bar Association. He took the most unselfish and deepest interest in advancing all these causes.

Long after his death, Storey is remembered for his relentless devotion to the causes that required his innate sense of justice. He may not have welcomed the idea of people calling him a reformist or philanthropist. Still, he was indeed both, in the noblest sense. He was the kind of person that took great delight in championing an unpopular cause. During his long life of service rendered to society, it would be difficult to name the most unselfish and devoted of his many areas of work. However, no estimate of his character and achievements and no memoir of his life would be complete without emphasizing his unrelenting labor for African Americans.

Undoubtedly, his intimate association with Charles Sumner as his private secretary and the confidences they shared during the years after the Civil War, which eventually culminated in President Johnson's impeachment, had a remarkable impact on his character as a young Harvard graduate. These were the influences that gave him the courage to become a great anti-slavery leader. Storey considered it his responsibility to preserve and defend the rights of African Americans that were already written in the federal constitution – at a very high cost. Just as Elijah's mantle fell on Elisha in the Bible, so also did Sumner's fifteenth amendment of the Constitution fall on Storey to defend. [2]

Although he had an extensive and exacting professional practice, his orderly and keen mind allowed him to be at the forefront of the Bar in his time and render immense service to move society forward. Storey's life was a long and fulfilled one. Still, most importantly, it was beneficial both to his colleagues at the Bar and the entire community where he once lived. His colleagues at the Bar described his unique personality and disregard for the possible consequences of advocating unpopular measures as an act that demonstrated John Adam's valuation of the opportunities of a lawyer:

> *"Integrity and skill at the bar are better supporters of independence than any fortune, talents, or eloquence elsewhere. A man of genius, talents, eloquence, integrity, and judgment at the bar is the most independent man in society. Presidents, governors, senators, judges have not so much honest liberty; but it ought always to be regulated by prudence and never abused."* [1]

Such an individual was Moorfield Storey. The following pages expand upon the events and accomplishments of Storey's life, including his fight for the rights of the oppressed, his activities while he was alive, and his beliefs. This collection of records describes his early days growing up, his family, his activities while he served in different capacities, and his challenges and victories.

EARLY LIFE

Who is Moorfield Storey? (1845)

O N MARCH 19, 1845, Moorfield Storey was born in Roxbury, Massachusetts, into a long-settled family. Although he wasn't wealthy, he was comfortable. He gained a sense of security which enabled him to chart an independent course. He inherited his tenacious adherence to the high principles that characterized his life from his abolitionist mother.

In 1866, Storey graduated from Harvard College and served briefly between 1867 and 1869 as the personal secretary to U.S. Senator Charles Sumner. He was admitted to the Bar in 1869 and later became a prominent Boston attorney. Storey got married to Gertrude Cutts in 1870 and entered private law practice in 1871. He was the president of the Bar Association of the City of Boston, Massachusetts, between 1909 and 1913. He was also the president of the Massachusetts Bar Association.[3,4]

As an undergraduate, Storey usually skipped classes to go fishing and partied into the early hours on other days. He left Harvard Law School in his second year to serve as private secretary to Massachusetts senator Charles Sumner. Sumner was popularly referred to as the South's most hated foe, the Negro's greatest friend, and as a man of absolute fidelity to principle and unflinching courage.

A look at his life and achievements shows that the influence of his mentor Charles Sumner was pivotal for the rest of his life.

Education and Friendship with the Emerson Family

According to the earliest recollections of Storey's younger sister Mariana Teresa in her book, *Family Recollections,* the siblings practically laid the foundations of a liberal education by keenly studying any book they could find and grabbing something tangible from it. One of the best sources of information for them was *Harper's Magazine.* Once they read all they could, they would eventually use it artistically and even paint the illustrations.

In the words of his younger sister, Storey was a meticulous pre-Raphaelite and a "wag" while growing up. She remembered him painting Napoleon in a bright yellow waistcoat as well as chocolate polka dots. He even painted the young lad who had tried to assassinate Napoleon in a chocolate waistcoat and yellow dots too. She recalls Storey cutting out paper dolls for her with square heads and round heads. When Mariana protested at what he did, he told her that they were blockheads, which was a sufficient explanation for the whole phenomenon. Then, when Storey stripped the doll of every feminine clothing, transformed her mantles into regal robes and her sashes into turbans, then finally named her the Sublime Porte, Mariana was left speechless with admiration.

They had Homer's *Iliad* with Flaxman's illustrations as well as a couplet from Pope's translation beneath each one. According to Mariana, apart from the original Greek, they knew that by heart and others, like *Arabian Nights* and *Pilgrim's Progress.* They would have even excelled in any creditable examination on the three great religions of the world.

Mariana described her brother as a quiet person full of fun and loved by everyone. He was not unusually fond of studying, but he was also never far from the head of his class in school. Storey possessed subtle energy, which he displayed throughout his life – he was often busy engaging his mind in things he wanted to do, whether play or work. Just like the rest of his siblings, Storey was an excellent reader, and he and his siblings were fondly called bookworms by their aunt Mary. Storey combined several qualities of his parents. He was much like his father in his mental ability and character, while he took after his mother's temperament and disposition.

According to a letter that Storey wrote for a class book, he spent the first eleven years in Roxbury before moving to Boston, where he settled for a long time. He secured a spot at the Latin public school in Boston, and the name of his principal was Gardner. In 1862, Storey entered the first-year class and occupied No. 8 College House with Charles B. Brigham in the first year. Subsequently, he occupied Nos. 32, 21, and 27 Massachusetts with John G. Curtis. He received college awards while in school, was a member of the Institute of 1770, Phi Beta Kappa, Hasty Pudding Club and Natural History Society, and was made the Class Orator. Storey was first on the rank list of scholarships for senior year and sixth for four years.

One of his friends recalled Storey's keen and delightful sense of humor, something never forgotten by his classmates. When they first met in 1857, Charles Edwin Stratton recalled in their first term as freshmen, they all agreed to learn more about each member of their divisions. On a particular occasion, they called on one of their classmates, who received them solemnly but kindly. Well, Storey was irrepressible, and after a few outbursts, their solemn classmate remarked, "Storey, your drollery is inimitable." They also never forgot to quote the words used by another leader of the Bar, a Japanese law student, who had this to say about Storey: "His pleasant says and merry tells."

In July 1866, one of the pictures found in the journal of Ralph Waldo Emerson shows the youthful Storey, Ralph Waldo Emerson, and Ellery Channing with four beautiful ladies and three boys. Storey, Edward Emerson, and Tom Ward had just graduated from Harvard and went camping on Monadnock.

Unfortunately, their fun was cut short by terrible weather with north wind and rain. Things were quite difficult as it was very cold in the evening, and the boys had to give out their blankets to the ladies and the elderly gentlemen who were with them. So, Storey and the other two boys spent the night keeping up the campfire. Storey, one of the outstanding members of the Harvard Glee Club, did not fail to entertain them by singing songs with Edward Emerson, to the great pleasure of the company. As the writer recalls, the two friends sang in the dark and cold for quite a long time, not just to keep up their courage but because Storey was courageous and cheerful enough for the entire company. [74,75]

Notable Achievements

One of the notable achievements Storey will be remembered for was a case before the Supreme Court in 1917 which overturned a segregation law in Louisville, Kentucky, based on property rights. In *Buchanan v. Warley,* he argued that the law violated property owners' rights to sell their homes to anyone they wanted.[6] A clear statement of Story's argument can be found in the Supreme Court ruling:

> *"...violates the Fourteenth Amendment of the Constitution of the United States, in that it abridges the privileges and immunities of citizens of the United States to acquire and enjoy property, takes property without due process of law, and denies equal protection of the laws."*

The views of the segregationists were also clearly described by the Court as follows:

> *"This drastic measure is sought to be justified under the authority of the State in the exercise of the police power. It is said such legislation tends to promote the public peace by preventing racial conflicts; that it tends to maintain racial purity; that it prevents the deterioration of property owned and occupied by white people, which deterioration, it is contended, is sure to follow the occupancy of adjacent premises by persons of color."*

As disgusting as the views of the segregationists were, Storey prevailed, and the law was overturned. This is a landmark victory for property rights, individual rights, and the libertarian lawyer Moorfield Storey. This ruling was also the first exception to state segregation laws and is presently regarded as a precursor to the *Brown v. Board of Education* ruling of 1945. According to law professor David Bernstein, this is one of the most significant civil rights cases decided before the modern civil rights era.[6]

Storey supported the mugwumps (independent politics and anti-imperialism) in the late 1800s. Also, as a reformer, he fought the mistreatment of Native Americans and political corruption. He became an outspoken critic of the mistreatment of immigrants, Jews, African Americans, Filipinos, and other persecuted groups. However, this did not in any way prevent his private practice from flourishing.

Throughout his career, Charles Sumner – who argued that segregation was unconstitutional and that the laws shouldn't make any racial distinctions as early as 1849 – significantly influenced Storey. Later, when southerners formalized the Jim Crow system of segregation, disfranchisement, and racial violence, Storey began to speak out against post-Reconstruction southern policies.[7]

The gathering of an inter-racial group in January 1909 in William English Walling's New York apartment was called to discuss proposals for an organization whose responsibility was to advocate for African Americans' civil rights and political rights. The group's nucleus included Mary White Ovington, William English Walling, and Henry Moskowitz. To obtain support, the group issued a call for a national conference on the anniversary of Abraham Lincoln's birth, February 12, 1909.

The call was made to all believers in democracy to participate in a national conference to discuss present evils, protest, and renew the struggle for civil and political liberty. *The Call* was written by Oswald Garrison Villard and sent to prominent white and black Americans for endorsement. There were sixty signers of *The Call*, and among them were Ida B. Wells, W.E.B Dubois, Francis J. Grimke, Mary Church Terrell, and Ray Stannard Baker.[8]

In response to the increasing trend of nationwide racial violence, Storey was part of the prominent group of Americans who responded to the invitation of Mary White Ovington to meet on February 12, 1909, to protest a recent race riot that took place in Abraham Lincoln's hometown of Springfield, Illinois, on the 100th anniversary of Lincoln's birth. This was also the same meeting that created the National

Association for the Advancement of Colored People (NAACP). Interestingly, Storey became the first president of the association in 1910 and occupied the position until he died.[7]

Although he had little to do with the day-to-day functioning of the NAACP, his legal skills were undoubtedly invaluable. Storey was a strong promoter of the idea that civil rights could be secured via the court easily and fought against the idea that the federal government couldn't prevent private discrimination.[7]

One of Storey's remarkable achievements was helping Lawrence Nixon prepare the brief for *Nixon v. Herndon* (1927) against the all-white primary. The Supreme Court ruled in this case that a 1923 Texas law had denied Nixon the right to vote in the Democratic primary unlawfully, primarily because of the color of his skin (this is a violation of the Fourteenth Amendment).

Interestingly, this case happens to be an integral part of the campaign against the white primary by the NAACP, and it ended in victory with *Smith v. Allwright* (1944). Some historians also believe that the successful campaign of the NAACP against segregation – outlawed by the *Brown v. Board of* Education U.S. Supreme Court decision of 1954 – was positively influenced by these victories won by Storey.[7]

> *"Between the principle of freedom, that all men are entitled to equal political rights, and the dogma of tyranny, that might makes right, there is no middle ground."*
> (Moorfield Storey, March 2, 1920)

Indeed, Storey was a fascinating man who deserves to be a central hero to libertarians. He was an opponent of protectionism, an advocate of gold, and a defender of depoliticized markets.[6]

His Father's Impact on his Social Life and Upbringing

Storey was friends with Ralph Waldo Emerson's son Edward Waldo Emerson for a long time. They were in the same graduating class at Harvard during the darkest moments of the Civil War. One may never know how Storey got the attention of Charles Sumner in the first place. But in his senior year, Storey led his class and was selected as a class orator. At the then unreformed Harvard Law School, the popular senator asked Storey to come to Washington as his private secretary at the end of the year.

Storey's father played a crucial role in his upbringing. As his son would remember, he was "the most perfect gentleman I ever knew... he had a brilliant mind, a marvelous memory, lover of good books and fine taste in literature." Storey's father's friends were James Russell Lowell, John Holmes, and Ebenezer Rockwood Hoar. He was often appreciated for his wit and was part of several social gatherings of his time and various distinguished clubs. Storey significantly benefited from his father's sociability, and this is how he met the most distinguished men of his time in Massachusetts.

Although many would easily assume that Storey was born into great wealth because of his easy movement and association in the world of the Boston Brahmins, that is not correct. One of the things that helped shape his political education was the ideas of the "Conscience Whigs." The group adopted this name on the day Hoar stood up in the Massachusetts State Senate to declare that the time had come for the legislature to represent the conscience of the Commonwealth and its cotton. John Gorham Palfrey, Charles Sumner, Hoar, and Charles Francis Adams were among the group members. The members, regardless of their partisan label between 1846 and 1861, were a group of individuals who made efforts to actualize abolitionist goals within the constitutional framework of the Whig.[9] Of course, the people we associate with often matter, and these men, in several ways, influenced him. He quickly gained a sense of security to chart an independent course. His abolitionist mother also played a crucial role in shaping his life and helping him adhere to the high principles that characterized him.

SENATOR CHARLES SUMNER AND MOORFIELD STOREY

C HARLES SUMNER ATTENDED Phillips Academy at Andover, and in 1796, he graduated from Harvard College, where he also established a cordial relationship with Storey's father, Charles Storey. This friendship eventually played a crucial role in Storey's life as Sumner influenced him greatly. Sumner was admitted as an attorney in 1801 and became actively interested in politics as a supporter of Jefferson. In 1804, his first political speech was an argument against disunion.

Between 1806-07 and 1810-11, Sumner was the clerk of the House of Representatives. He was a powerful orator, an American Statesman, an academic lawyer, and the United States Senator from Massachusetts. He was not just a leader of the Radical Republicans in the U.S. Senate but was also at the forefront of the fight against slavery in the state. As the anti-slavery coalitions rose and fell in the 1830s and 1840s, Sumner had to switch political parties several times before joining the Republican Party in the 1850s. He focused mainly on demolishing what Republicans regarded as "Slave Power," which refers to the influence of southern slave owners over the federal government as they made efforts to ensure the expansion and continuation of slavery.

Sumner was almost killed with a cane on the Senate floor by a South Carolina Democratic congressman, Preston Brooks. His offense was that he delivered an anti-slavery speech titled *The Crime Against Kansas*. While delivering his speech, Sumner described the first cousin of his attacker, Senator Andrew Butler from South Carolina, as a pimp for slavery. The incident was serious and even though it made both men famous, it left Sumner severely wounded.

He could not return to the Senate for several years, and his desk in the Senate was always left empty to remind others of the incident. He was eventually reelected, but the incident was part of the factors that significantly polarized the country, culminating in the Civil War. In Storey's view, Sumner was "the South's most hated foe and the Blacks' greatest friend." According to Storey:

"Charles Sumner was a great man in his absolute fidelity to principle, his clear perception of what his country needed, his unflinching courage, his perfect sincerity, his persistent devotion to duty, his indifference to selfish considerations, his high scorn of anything petty or mean.

He was essentially simple to the end, brave, kind, and pure.... Originally modest and not self-confident, the result of his long contest was to make him egotistical and dogmatic. There are few successful men who escape these penalties of success, the common accompaniment of increasing years...

Sumner's naively simple nature, his confidence in his fellows, and his lack of humor combined to prevent his concealing what many feel but are better able to hide. From the time he entered public life till he died, he was a strong force constantly working for righteousness... To Sumner more than to any single man, except possibly Lincoln, the colored race owes its emancipation and such measure of equal rights as it now enjoys."

Storey's biography of Sumner is best described as a sympathetic and thoughtful narrative of the career of his former employer. He provided an accurate record of Sumner's mental and moral traits and his deficiencies and virtues. Storey gave Sumner full credit for his solid and sincere advocacy of the radical principles of the anti-slavery reform while disclosing the fact that Sumner was not very successful in gaining the approval of his associates in public life.[10,11]

Charles Sumner's Influence on Moorfield Storey

In his time, Charles Sumner was among the most outspoken opponents of slavery; he never stopped being a strong advocate for freed African Americans, even after the Civil War. Having lived with and observed Sumner for about two years, Storey also derived his belief that we live our lives and make our wrongs right in terms of inflexible moral principles.

Among most American statesmen of his time, Sumner made a remarkable impact as the most committed advocate of civil rights for the freed individuals in the U.S. while serving as chairman of the Senate Foreign Relations Committee. But Sumner's life also influenced Storey significantly while he was Sumner's secretary. Storey imbibed the humanitarian concerns and the moralistic approach to politics of the Conscience Whigs of Massachusetts. But the brain behind his clerkship with Sumner was Charles Storey, his father.

Although Storey's father seems to have political traits like those of the Conscience Whigs, he was still part of the party until 1850. But according to his son, his father eventually left because of his displeasure at Webster's support of the Fugitive Slave Law. So as Storey would remember, by 1856, his father became the "Sumner Republican" and introduced his son to the anti-slavery senator.

At the time, Sumner was recovering from a defeat he suffered at the hands of a self-appointed defender of Southern honor. Charles Storey sent his son a letter informing him that Mr. Edward L. Pierce and Mr. F. V. Balch had talked about Storey taking over the position of secretary to Mr. Sumner. The latter was happy with what he had heard about him. At the time, Storey was already yearning to escape from his second year at Harvard Law School.

He was thinking of signing on as a ship's clerk, so when Storey received the offer, he gladly accepted it immediately. He arrived in Washington in late November 1867 and was the senator's secretary and clerk to the Foreign Relations Committee. Interestingly, most of the tasks assigned to him were a bit challenging. He took over the vacant room in Sumner's house at the beginning of January 1868, and every morning he would meet with the petitioners downstairs. In those days, they were the ones who often occupied most of the homes of their congressmen before congressional office buildings ever existed.

One of the tasks Storey handled for Sumner was to answer most of his correspondence. At some point, Storey complained to his roommates back in college about replying to different people. In his words:

> *"Whose views, doubtless of importance in Los Lunas, N. Mexico, or S. Malden, Mass., seem hardly to have the same weight here or materially affect the national policy."*

Even from his humble position, the impressionable twenty-three-year-old Storey had the chance to be involved in the excitement of Washington society. One event he would never forget was a dinner party organized by Sumner for Charles Dickens. Storey and War Secretary Edwin Stanton's secretary were the only guests present at the dinner. Despite other people's opinions about Sumner, Storey greatly admired his ideals and career.

While Storey was still a clerk, one of the most remarkable events in Washington was the congressional impeachment proceedings against President Andrew Johnson. While the argument in the House mainly focused on the President's violation of some restrictions on his power of appointment, the final break led to two years of serious disagreement between the Republicans and Johnson in Congress.

Unsurprisingly, Johnson – a committed Democrat and a supporter of the small farmers of Tennessee – did not show any interest in the Republican party's continued supremacy, like Lincoln, and did not share Lincoln's growing acceptance of the idea that former slaves should be granted some civil rights. Johnson went ahead to restore self-governance to Confederate states that were defeated, leading to Republican anxiety that there would be an increase in Southern representation in Congress because of the abolition of the Constitution's three-fifths clause. This further increased the emerging opposition of the North to what appeared to be efforts to return the Blacks to their former servitude.

Johnson's attitude toward the freedmen and the South eventually turned the Northern opinion against him. Consequently, Republican moderates were pushed toward the Radicals, the most militant party members. This eventually led to several outcomes: the passage of the Fourteenth Amendment, guaranteeing citizenship to all Americans, and the imposition of Black suffrage on the Southern states as terms for their return to the Union.

Also, it resulted in the impeachment proceedings, which had never before been initiated against a U.S. President. Storey was not happy about the conflict between Congress and Johnson. He accused Johnson of usurping power in a letter he wrote to his father and specifically attacked him for his frequent reference to "Africanization" if the freedmen were granted civil rights. Storey referred to his actions as "an abominable appeal to prejudice."

Amid these issues between Johnson and the Congress, Sumner was head of the Radicals in the Senate, as earlier mentioned. When it came to the fight against Johnson, Sumner was a major force, and in Storey's opinion the senator's personality was not touched by the foul play in Congress. On the other hand, it would be inappropriate to conclude that Storey idolized Sumner since, as he clearly remarked regarding Sumner's idiosyncrasies after moving into his house:

> *"Mr. Sumner is not great at conversations, properly so-called, I think. He can make himself very agreeable if he likes and frequently does, but he either does all the talking himself and goes off into long disquisitions, or he simply draws out the other person and lets him do the talking, so it is a monologue on one side or the other."*

Being a man desperately searching for friendship (beyond the calculated associations of official Washington), Sumner found Storey to be his daily companion after several months. Perhaps one of the minor controversies of American historiography is the extent to which Sumner was without friends – whether he was the cause of it or not. One thing was clear. Sumner had a genuine affection for Storey, and this affection was also reciprocated. Fifty years later, Storey wrote, "I recall too many instances of his kindly thought for myself and others not to feel that his essential nature has been much represented."

Storey missed a few chances to defend Sumner against several criticisms that tarnished his reputation. He conceded that Sumner had certain flaws in his biography of Sumner, which he wrote as part of the Houghton Mifflin American Statesmen series:

> *"He was a man of great ability but not of the highest intellectual power, nor was he a master of style. He was not incisive in thought or speech. His orations were overloaded, his rhetoric was often turgid, he was easily led into irrelevance and undue stress upon undisputed points. His untiring industry as a reader had filled his memory with associations which perhaps he valued unduly. Originally modest and not self-confident, the result of his long contest was to make him egotistical and dogmatic."*

Storey was still willing to say this and even more about Sumner, and it is not easy to brush aside the views of someone who lived in the same house with his subject and saw his subject daily. The summary of Storey's opinion about Sumner is that his weaknesses overshadowed his virtues. Storey said, "Sumner was by nature essentially simple, affectionate, sincere, and kind. According to a classmate, Sumner was possessed by a life-and-death earnestness."

Storey's preparation to begin his career appeared to be complete when it was finally time to leave Washington in the spring of 1869. After receiving quality education from the Latin School and Harvard College, it was clear that he had acquired the best education Boston could offer. Since he had previously directed Storey's preparation for the Bar examination, Sumner went further by helping him get a job as Assistant District Attorney for Suffolk County.

Most of the men Storey and his generation saw as their models and wanted to emulate (individuals who believed in their principles and refused to compromise) were gradually ending their lives in political isolation while Storey kicked off the practice of law. During this period, Hoar and Adams were defeated in elections while Sumner, who was not on good terms with the Grant administration, was not granted his chairmanship by his Senate colleagues.

As described in *The Crisis*, Storey insisted there was much to say about Sumner having lived in the closest intimacy with him. Storey remarked that pointing out the evils caused by Black suffrage was easy, but if Black suffrage had been refused, we would have recorded far greater evils.

Here is how the author of *Life of Sumner* (John T. Morse) described Storey's response: "Whether his (Storey's) attachment to his former employer made him biased, I'm not wise enough to pronounce. But all friends of Storey would confirm it when I say that Storey's loyalty to Charles Sumner's memory was part of his winning qualities." He confirmed failing to induce Storey to admit that his former employer was arrogant in a private conversation.

At some point, one of Storey's closest friends wrote that Sumner was overbearing, always had a constant air of superiority, and was vain and conceited. Storey did not hesitate to respond to his remark:

"I lived with him for two years and used his library while he received visitors of every race, color and rank. At that stage in my life when I was very young, I was quite sensitive to affections of superiority, but the way Mr. Sumner's received his visitors struck me with gracious courtesy."

Although he was no respecter of persons, he exuded kind and natural manners. To better understand Sumner's influence on the young Storey, it is imperative to look beyond a secretary's affectionate loyalty to his employer. When Storey met Sumner, it could best be described as a turning point for young Storey's career. So, at the time, he completely accepted Sumner's doctrine that in all political and social questions, the main issue is whether the question is right or wrong.

One of the things that Sumner taught Storey was to repeat the Romans, saying, "Where liberty is, there is my party." Storey seems to have had a Roman mind, a practical intelligence, and an ethical temperament instead of a mysterious or religious one. Sumner's principles and examples gave Storey the mindset that every high-minded American should endeavor to help fellow citizens secure and maintain their rights. Storey's stay in Washington was also memorable because he met the high-spirited and lovely Miss Gertrude, who later became his wife in 1870.[12,11]

Moorfield Storey, Pattern of the Intellectual Rebel (1884....)

One of the best pieces of content out there that revealed who Storey was and the impact he left behind after his life on earth is the biography by M.A. De Wolfe Howe in *Pattern of the Intellectual Rebel.* Storey was described as one of the "incarnations of the national conscience" of nineteenth-century America. His perfection was also viewed to be exceptional, and he played a vital role in history as well as in how we now see American life. Many individuals curious about the key elements of American thought will undoubtedly study the role Storey played in shaping American opinion.

Although his intellectual prowess was mainly nineteenth century, it also extended into the twentieth century and has not ceased to exist. He was the same intellectual rebel even after the current of thought veered over to focus more on causes commonly regarded by its proponents as "liberalism," while those against it called it parlor socialism. Storey's type of intellectual rebellion is best viewed as the "mugwump" type. The term "mugwump" was used temporarily to describe Republicans who bolted Blaine's nomination for president, which means it is not a perfect description but something close.

According to General Horace Porter's definition of the word mugwump, when it was first used in 1884, *"A mugwump is someone who is educated beyond his intellect."* Regardless of how correct that definition may be, one thing is sure – Storey personified it above everyone else.

He had always been rebellious and many who knew him would easily predict his subsequent actions even before he took them. For instance, it was apparent that Storey – who was also described as the perfect mugwump – would not support the war with Spain. He also opposed every form of tariff bill, the annexation of the Philippines, and often fought for the social equality of the African Americans.

But Storey as an individual appears not to have any historical importance. As a private citizen, perhaps the only attention he attracted was that of his fellow mugwumps. He rose high enough in his profession to become the American Bar Association's president. Also, he was an officer of different reform organizations, was once the president of the Massachusetts Reform Club, and twice an overseer of Harvard College. Most of the pamphlets he wrote focused mainly on his hobbies, and his last reform presidency was that of the NAACP.

As mentioned earlier, Storey's entrance into public affairs was as Senator Charles Sumner's secretary. Perhaps one primary reason he did not spread his wings of rebellion at the time was because of his likeness with his chief. But a look at Storey's letters during this period reveals that he was eager to see President Johnson impeached and removed from office. He wanted Johnson to be deprived of his powers immediately, without any trial.

His letters reveal his views, and at this point, Storey was on the side of the majority while complaining bitterly of their incompetence at taking advantage of opportunities that should be used as weapons against the president. In Mr. Howe's opinion, as expressed in the biography, Storey had an instinct for unpopular causes, and that instinct survived even though modern intellectualism had taken a different direction. Presently, its focus is on social betterment and not on every isolated topic we encounter daily.

For instance, Storey immediately got involved in conventions and mass meetings when the McKinley Administration decided to annex the Philippines, unlike what the liberals would do today. The liberals would move in their numbers to the Kentucky mining regions in response to a social conflict in their quest to demonstrate – by their gesture – the inequality of the social system. This indicates the difference between the mugwump prototypes and the liberals who appear to pursue every isolated purpose.

They move to any location in the news, demonstrating that they are not interested in a particular cause but focused on what is publicized. This differs significantly from Storey's approach, and even though it is not extinct, it has mostly given way to modern intellectualism in

American history. According to Henry Adams, while writing to Storey in 1912:

> *"I am fairly knocked out, but I imagine that you are still in the ring and as long as you can stand, you will enjoy loathing somebody."*

Indeed, Storey was a mugwump to the highest degree and remained in the ring, sending punches even after 80 years. He spent most of the latter part of his years fighting for the Filipinos and African Americans, with all the arsenals at his disposal. We can look at one of Storey's sayings to get an idea of his state of mind regarding a passionate cause, the African Americans. While visiting Hampton Institute and New York, Storey wrote to Teresa, his younger sister:

> *"I was touched by the warm expressions of regard which all the colored people who spoke to me uttered. I was complimented far beyond my desserts, but one does not cherish malice against flatterers, and I think they meant what they said."*

What exactly were the flatteries and compliments Storey was referring to in his letter that were "far beyond his desserts?" It is most likely that the only one he quoted was also the one he regarded as the highest compliment:

> *"A colored man expressed surprise when I met him; he had always supposed Moorfield was a Black man and he certainly meant that."*

His conclusion reveals how sincerely delighted he was, and this incident shows the mindset of the rebel against whatever he was interested in. Even more revelatory is the public address of William Lloyd Garrison, where he declared, *"I am ashamed of my own color."* According to Mr. Howe, it was Storey's glory that partisanship was alien to him and that he could freely align himself with any cause that was genuinely entitled to his respect and support. Commonly called the "independent," this is perhaps where the accuracy of the word is questioned.

All mugwumps and Mr. Howe assumed that an independent would undoubtedly vote in a specific way in a bid to prove a point against the boss. They failed to understand that many independents and individuals who have no party ties will often vote for candidates of the boss and the machine. They frequently do this when they have sincerely examined the advantages of the case and concluded that in that specific instance – and the case of the election – voting for the machine's candidates and the boss would be the best thing to do.

So, it would be in the best interest that Tammany Hall or the Vare machine in Philadelphia should oversee the government instead of the irresponsible ticket nominated by the reformers. But years of studying the cause of elections have shown the writer of this biography that such independents who are highly concerned about civic welfare, just like every mugwump, are in greater number and even more influential than the mugwumps.

The revelations of the mugwumps' remarkable role in American life and history have far more psychological value to the U.S. now. One striking instance of Storey's personality was when he took sides against Sacco and Vanzetti. One would have easily concluded that the temperamental rebel would quickly take sides with the accused men. But as Mr. Howe pointed out in his book:

> *"The accused men were not of a race like Filipino or African American from which Moorfield has a strong conviction that his country was depriving them of civil rights and liberties."*

He further speculated that Storey would have taken the sides of Sacco and Vanzetti if they had been Filipinos or African Americans. Although Mr. Howe did not say so, he believed Storey would have done so because that is how the mugwump's mind works. The liberal mind works differently; they all supported Sacco and Vanzetti since such cases serve as an opportunity to clarify their theme, which is the injustice of the social system. He concluded by adding that the final trait of the mugwump is complete fairness and freedom from bias in all subjects. [13]

Although Storey was influenced by many of his father's associates, the most remarkable role in shaping his beliefs was Charles Sumner. Sumner had earlier established a good relationship with Storey's father, and this friendship must have been instrumental to his association with the senator. Sumner made several efforts to ensure that Southern slave owners did not influence the federal government and continue the expansion of slavery. It was not surprising that Storey would also continue the fight against racism and violence, just like Sumner did.

It is interesting to note that Storey's father was against slavery, and he did not hesitate to introduce his son to Sumner, who was regarded as the anti-slavery senator. So, Storey must have embraced his father's beliefs regarding African American slaves at the time, and this ideology was further reinforced when he served as secretary to Sumner. While serving as chairman of the Senate Foreign Relations Committee, Sumner was a strong advocate of civil rights for freed persons in the U.S. Undoubtedly, Sumner's influence on Storey was far beyond affectionate loyalty to his employer. While writing Sumner's biography, Storey quickly acknowledged that Sumner was the source of his strong and sincere advocacy of the radical principles of the anti-slavery reforms. He was quick to align himself with causes that genuinely deserved his respect and support, which explains why he always freely expressed his opposing views against racial violence and other forms of oppression.

PROFESSIONAL LIFE

Obedience of the Law (1889...)

MOORFIELD STOREY'S ADDRESS at the opening of Petigru College in Columbia, South Carolina, has been identified by scholars as very relevant. They believe that it is part of the knowledge base of civilization as we know it. While addressing his audience, Storey did not fail to register his happiness over the occasion, which was the dedication of a new building for teachers of the law. In his words:

"There never was a time in the history of the world when it was more crucial to teach the knowledge and respect for the law."

He gave the address at a time when autocracy and its strongholds in Austria, Germany, Turkey, and Russia had been overthrown, which was immediately after the end of the war. The war brought untold hardship to many countries and resulted in increased rates of violence. Those who took part in it came back bitter after experiencing horrors, and some of them had been brutalized. Some of them now hated their fellow citizens who were at home earning large wages or profiting from their businesses while they risked their lives with insignificant pay.

The United States and other countries faced a disbanded army that contained several dangerous elements, and Storey believed it was time to make the world safe for democracy. He talked about what the "law" meant and why it was important at the time, adding that when people violate the law with impunity, there will be chaos and an increase of barbaric acts. On the other hand, he believed that a community that obeys and enforces the law will be regarded as a civilized one.

The rule of civilization is that an impartial tribunal (a board of arbitration created by all parties, or a court established by law) should decide any dispute. He reminded his audience that the United States might face the consequences of anarchy if the citizens fail to work toward restoring the supremacy of law in deciding the outcome of disputes between employees and employers.

Another issue that Storey addressed was the cases of lynching taking place in the U.S. The level of lynching in the United States was alarming, and he was concerned that if nothing was done about it, things could worsen. He noted that about 3,224 individuals had lost their lives between 1889 and 1918. Storey lamented the silence of the enlightened men who watched American citizens carry out cruel executions of human beings, torturing them and sometimes burning them at the stake. While many justify such inhumane acts as a punishment meant for people who commit certain offenses, such justification lacks a foundation.

Storey observed that African Americans who were killed by the mob were only charged or suspected of committing a crime, and in some cases, some of them were innocent individuals. When someone is charged, the court presumes that they are innocent until proven guilty of the crimes they are charged with. But a mob concludes that the charge is proof of a person's guilt in a crime.

While referring to the words of Henry Watterson, Storey added that lynching was no longer an attempt to punish those who committed a crime but some form of sport that justifies its actions based on an offense of greater or less gravity. Some individuals who engage in it often do so because of the law's delays or failures. Also, some of them simply want to have a good time carrying out such inhumane acts even when they are not drunk.

What seemed to be of major concern to Storey was that such crimes continued to happen unchecked, and those involved in them had not been punished for several years. Most of these lynchings took place in communities where men of character and influence had what it would take to ensure that the law was enforced and make those involved in such acts outcasts in the community, eventually discouraging the ugly trend.

Storey was also concerned about the impact of the lynchings on children who saw such barbaric acts, along with their mothers. He pointed out that the children watching such barbarities would eventually grow up and govern the country in a few years, so how would they govern the country? He described barbarism as an enemy that is worse than fire or flood and how it threatens the entire nation's civilization and should be eliminated. Since African Americans were taxed, drafted into the military of the United States, and had sacrificed their properties and lives during the war, their loyalty could not be questioned.

But it was impossible to enforce all the obligations of about 12 million citizens of the United States without also giving them rights. He believed that there would be disastrous consequences for any country that permanently denied people their rights. In his view, a safe community is one where an injury to even the poorest citizen is seen as an injury to the state. One of the strong cases Storey made for the fair treatment of Black employees was the impact of the World War. The war resulted in the loss of lives in Europe and a significant drop in the workforce.

This, he believed, would compel most European countries to restrict their citizens from migrating to other countries like the United States. While this was happening in Europe, he added that the United States was going to enjoy a season of prosperity and abundance since, at the time, the U.S. was the only country that had what it would take to supply the needs of Europe. The war had already affected England, France, and Germany, and the European population's needs had increased remarkably. Considering these circumstances, having a contented workforce was essential, and the North could attract the labor needed to prosper since Northern employers offered higher wages. Unfortunately, if the North failed to stop the menace of mob lynching, then the labor required to take advantage of these opportunities would be discouraged.

Storey strongly believed that, at first, those who suffered the consequences of condoning lawlessness were the weak and lowly in society. But things were gradually changing as the elite began to face new threats, like the use of mail bombs loaded with explosives being sent to leading men in the country and to a justice of the Supreme Court of the United States. In his opinion, one effective way to avert such disasters from occurring was to refrain from allowing the abuses of human rights. Storey believed that every citizen must get justice and enjoy equal opportunity. Every citizen (and not just whites and African Americans) should be given equal rights. Storey urged his audience to consider that the lynching of individuals in the United States must cease to disgrace the good name of the country and concluded by quoting the words of President Roosevelt:

"The corner-stone of this republic, as of all free governments, is respect for and obedience to the law. Where men permit the law to be defied or evaded, whether by rich man or poor man, by black men or white (and may I interpolate, by President or private citizen), we are by just so much weakening the bonds of our civilization and increasing the chances of its overthrow and of the substitution therefore of a system in which there shall be violent alterations of anarchy and tyranny."[14,15]

The Present Position of the Independent Man (1891)

While speaking before the Harvard Reform Club in Sanders Theatre, Storey reviewed all the promises made by the Democratic and Republican parties regarding tariff reform, elections, civil service reform, and honest money. He also explained how each of these parties failed to fulfill their promises. But his view regarding President Cleveland's administration was different, and according to Storey:

"The administration of President Cleveland shows the strength and weakness of Democratic civil service reform. His administration was not a civil service administration. He found a civil service founded on the spoils system for twenty-five years and it was a tremendous force for one man to resist. He was not supported by his party and this fact merely shows that a civil service reformer can pin his faith to neither party... the hope of tariff reformers seems to be with the Democracy."

Storey believed that, based on the speeches made by Republican leaders, they saw the McKinley bill as a step forward which would soon be followed by other measures. When it came to the silver issue, he believed that Grover Cleveland was one man whose opinion was dearest, strongest, and never doubted. However, the silver question was not a party question, since there were anti-silver and free-silver men in the Republican and Democratic parties. He believed that no party could be implicitly trusted regarding four questions – honest money, civil service reform, honest election, and tariff reform.

Storey wondered if there was a way they could use their power of discretion. He referred to a military idea of politics provided by ex-Governor Brackett which painted the picture of the two parties as a group of individuals standing like hostile armies, each supporting their standard-bearer (who is also their respective candidate) and going against their enemy "blindly." Since they are charging against the foe, they have thrown aside all arguments regarding the character of the standard bearer and what they all focus on is blind devotion. He believed that this was the kind of doctrine that produced the likes of the Platts, Gormans, Hills, and Dudleys.

But an independent voter is free to vote for any good man who believes as he does, so whenever he acts as an outstanding Democrat or Republican, he eventually weakens the hands of the bad individuals in the parties. While making a case for the independent man, Storey adds that the independent man travels through several states and votes for any candidate of choice – Republican or Democratic – based on the party they feel is better in each state. For instance, he could be for the Republicans in Maryland and for the Democrats in Virginia. It would be the case of "choosing the lesser of two evils" in Ohio and New York.

However, the moment the Massachusetts line is crossed, all doubts should fade, and the course of the independents should be clear. Undoubtedly, the governor of Massachusetts had provided a practical display of civil service reform, and Storey believed that the administration could not be attacked because this was proven a few days ago. He asked that since many Independents, Democrats and Republicans believed in the same things, why were they not united? In his view, those who kept men of all parties asunder were the rascals of both the Republican and Democratic parties.

He believed that members of all parties who shared the same beliefs should meet the following spring and explore ways to organize and get encouraged by one another when they get in contact with each other, just as soldiers are usually encouraged by the touch of elbows. Of course, he was confident that such a gathering of men who shared the same beliefs – regardless of the party they belong to – and who desired to see the progress of the United States, would not be ignored by any party; instead, both parties would desire them. He finally concluded by adding that any party that would open their arms to such a group of individuals and embrace their desires would eventually become an outstanding party. However, if the Republican and Democratic parties continued to follow their wrong ways, then the emergence of a new party was inevitable.[16] It is interesting to note that Storey's last statement revealed the events before the founding of the NDP a few years later, as we would later find out.[16]

Moorfield Storey Assails Brandeis for Wreck of Road (1892)

The Senate sub-committee considered Louis D. Brandeis of Boston's nomination for the bench of the Supreme Court of the U.S. On this occasion, Storey spoke under oath to the Senate sub-committee of how Brandeis brought suits that resulted in the wrecking of the New York & New England Road and subsequent acquisition by New Haven company before he started his campaign against the New Haven Railroad.

Storey explained to the sub-committee members that in the suits against the New England Railroad, Brandeis claimed to work for a Boston liquor dealer known as Goldsmith, a minor stockholder in New England. But it was later discovered during the trial of directors of the New Haven Road that Goldsmith received $27,000 as payment for expenses, and New Haven also paid an additional amount of $10,000 in a subsequent dispute regarding the use of Goldsmith's name.

As some observers noticed, Brandeis suffered another blow with the friendly testimony of Sherman L. Whipple, who was also a Boston lawyer. In the statement, Whipple commended President Wilson for choosing Brandeis. While ensuring a proper presentation of Brandeis's side of the case to the sub-committee, Mr. Anderson, the Federal District Attorney of Boston, described Storey as the head of the Boston Bar. He also described Whipple as New England's greatest litigating lawyer.

Whipple proceeded to read out the details of an interview which he granted members of the press where he praised what he described as the unselfish service of Brandeis for fighting the cause of the less fortunate of humanity. He further added that the highly criticized opinion of Brandies was what made him extremely useful in the Supreme Court. While explaining the role played by Brandeis in the Lennox case, Whipple informed the sub-committee that he thought that as far as the practice of the profession was concerned, Brandeis had followed a mistaken course with the purest motives.

Whipple explained that James Lennox of P. Lennox & Co (that was financially embarrassed) had a conference with one of the company's creditors, where he was advised to hire a counsel. He also entered the conference with three lawyers and retained Brandeis. While adhering to the advice given by Brandeis, Lennox assigned assets to Brandeis's law partner. Shortly after this, Brandeis's firm brought involuntary bankruptcy proceedings against the Lennox company as representatives of the creditors because Lennox had made the assignment as advised by Brandeis.

Even though four witnesses agreed that Lennox had retained Brandeis, Brandeis denied ever representing him. The testimony provided by Whipple and Storey made a remarkable impression on the sub-committee. However, the sub-committee had a few questions regarding Storey's summary of the opinion of the Boston Bar concerning the untrustworthiness of Brandeis in the efforts of New Haven to acquire the New England Railroad. While the Republican members appeared satisfied with Whipple's narrative of the Lennox case, the Democratic members questioned him and, in the process, allowed Whipple to express his personal belief that the entire case did not affect Brandeis's integrity.

While sharing his testimony regarding the New Haven's acquisition of the New England Railroad, Storey explained to the members of the sub-committee that the New Haven Railroad, in the Spring of 1892, undertook to eliminate the New England Railroad as their competitor. In the same year, while acting on behalf of Goldsmith, Brandeis brought several suits that were meant to affect the operations and finances of the New England Road.

Among the total of ten suits was one that prevented the payment of preferred dividends, and a second one was to stop the issuance of bonds. A third suit was focused on attacking leases and franchises. In the Spring of 1893, the Massachusetts legislature appointed a committee to examine the relations between the two companies at the instance of some produce dealers. Storey added that he conducted the hearings and stated that Brandeis testified to be the suits' counsel. The outcome of the suits resulted in the halting of the credit and earnings of New England Road. Later, in the fall of 1893, a receivership was established from which it became a part of New Haven.

Storey explained to the sub-committee that while investigating the case, he attempted to know who Brandeis was truly representing, and Brandeis testified that his client was Goldsmith. Unfortunately, when Storey asked who was paying the bills, Brandeis refused to answer him. Instead, he wanted an assurance that if he provided the information, the committee must not use his testimony in any other suit, but the committee declined Brandeis's request.

It was later discovered that Goldsmith owned sixty shares of New England stock valued at $3,000 and hadn't the financial resources to offset the cost of employing a counsel for six months. Obviously, the name of Goldsmith was chosen as the plaintiff before the suits after a careful look at the list of shareholders. Goldsmith was promised a reasonable amount of money if he would allow his name to be used. Storey added that he believes the individual behind the suits was a New York lawyer known as William J. Kelly. Although Kelly appeared to have lost interest in the suits in the fall of 1892, Olling Webb and

Morehouse appealed directly to the New Heaven Road, and subsequently, the suits were in New Haven's name.

He summarized that it was apparent the suits had malicious intentions of affecting the New England Road. Storey concluded that Brandeis's clients were not Goldsmith and Kelly, and he never regarded them as his clients. Instead, Brandeis was getting his orders from someone outside, that might have been Austin Corbin of New York, who was then president of the Long Island Railroad. He also suggested that Brandeis's client might have also been New Haven Road or a party that was or was not interested in New England Road. Regardless of the presence of the real person behind the suits, one thing was clear: the person wanted to destroy New England Road.

What bothered Storey, which he said he found difficult to understand, was the reason why Mr. Brandeis brought a bill in the name of individuals who were not his real clients without also being aware of the destruction such a suit would cause to the credit of New England Railroad. He noted that Goldsmith was later paid $27,000 for expenses during the trial of New Haven's directors, based on an agreement for New Haven to continue with the suits against New England Road.

The Goldsmith estate filed a suit against the Corbin estate after Austin Corbin's death, claiming a liberal compensation was promised to Goldsmith for using his name in the suits. Eventually, New Haven Railroad settled this action for $10,000. The chairman of the sub-committee asked Storey if he considered the conduct of Mr. Brandeis unethical. In his response, Storey told him that he did. The chairman proceeded to ask if Storey filed a complaint before the Bar Association, which Storey did not do. When the sub-committee asked what Mr. Brandeis's reputation was in Boston, Storey replied:

"Is that of a shrewd man, and able lawyer, energetic, not scrupulous, as to his methods and not to be trusted. I don't mean that he did not pay his debts." [17]

Time to Check Corruption (1894)

In his address, Storey focused on the tendency of legislative bodies in the United States to seek absolute power as the people were increasingly losing faith in the honesty of public men. While reading the annual address during the American Bar Association's meeting on August 23, 1894, Storey was quick to talk about the change in the relationship between the legislatures and the people and other dangers that have threatened the Republic through bribery and corruption of officeholders. He acknowledged that Americans enjoyed enormous material prosperity beyond historical precedent brought up with an abiding faith in the good sense of the citizens and the free institutions.

He did not mention the citizens' confidence that, regardless of the challenges they may be facing at the time, at least the future of the United States was secure. This assurance came from the knowledge that they cultivated a philosophic indifference to all political issues and the belief that when things get worse, then they could easily apply the remedy. But he believed every American must occasionally have noticed some tendencies occurring more frequently in recent years – due to several changes taking place in theories of government – and understood that they could not afford to ignore such issues.

He reminded his audience that all men were born free and equal and were entitled to certain essential, natural, and inalienable rights. Storey interpreted this declaration as implying that all individuals were free to work for anyone that agreed to hire them for any specific wage they decided to take and could make any legal contract as well as have legal use of their hands and properties. But what troubled him was that a good number of persons who were not interested in working also insisted that others should not work in their places. So, any person who wanted to follow a particular trade must first become a member of a workers' union or an association they formed. Such persons would have to submit their liberty to the control of such associations or abandon their desire to work.

Also, if a man failed to employ them based on their terms, then such an individual or organization should not hire someone else. The challenges faced by the legislature were also another issue Storey raised in his address. He cited instances of the difficulties faced by the legislature and gave an example of Connecticut, which was paralyzed for its entire term and could not even pass a single law. At the same time, the election was canceled, and the term of a Governor who was supposed to retire along with other state officers was extended for two more years without the legislature's consent.

Also, he gave instances of the challenges faced by the legislature in Rhode Island, Kansas, and New Jersey and decried the fact that such distasteful practices did not happen in Mexico or South America but in the oldest states of the U.S. and Kansas, where New England men predominantly settled.

To Storey, it may be said that both the illegal acts of desperate politicians and the unlawful actions of striking employees were periodic manifestations of lawlessness that often got the backlash of public opinion. He firmly believed that true character is shown not by how people commit crimes within the community but by how people regard and punish such crimes. He drew the attention of his audience to the change in the attitude of the citizens toward another vital principle of popular government.

The long struggle for free institutions eventually ended when Cornwallis surrendered, and the famous legislature was finally seen by many to serve as an adequate safeguard against arbitrary power. For instance, it was the States-General and National Assembly against the King and the nobles in France; in England, it was the Parliament. He informed his audience that their fathers fought against taxation without representation, and the outcome of what they fought for was the right to be governed by representatives of their choice, and their creed was clearly stated in the Massachusetts bill of rights:

"The Legislature ought frequently to assemble for the redress of grievances, for correcting, strengthening, and confirming the laws and for making new laws, as the common good may require."

However, Storey lamented that their descendants did not share the faith of their ancestors, starting from the legislative body in the United States and Senate down to the Aldermen of New York. The citizens were even ashamed of their representatives, who they frequently feared and distrusted. Also, the business community in the United States was not left out, as they accepted the adjournment of Congress as the end of a season that was faced with dread and perplexity. This distrust is also reflected in the legislature itself. He reminded them of the testimony given in New York before a legislature committee that revealed a community where both the legislature and the administration of the law had been for sale.

He decried the cases where criminals and even reputable men of wealth paid the law officers to neglect the discharge of their duty for many years. Also, prominent individuals and corporate organizations had given politicians large sums of money to enjoy legislative favors or insure themselves against hostile laws. On the other hand, humble peddlers ended up paying for the rights to earn a living.

In the richest and greatest city in the U.S., the government of laws had ceased to exist, and what replaced it was a government of corruption and blackmail. Fortunately, New York had enough virtue to start a reform process. Storey believes the state had learned a lesson that honest men often fail to realize sufficiently – how essentially and necessarily weak the combination of scoundrels is. To back up his statement, he referred to the fate of the Tweed Ring – which he believed was the most firmly entrenched conspiracy against good governance to ever exist in the U.S. – and the humiliating overthrow of McKane and his associates in crime was proof of what was possible.

He did not fail to reassure his audience that he was not an alarmist, adding that he had faith in common sense, virtue, and the political sagacity of the citizens. However, these qualities needed to assert themselves. Although he agreed with the view of others that when things become so terrible, they shall identify and apply the remedy, he wondered if things were not bad enough. Storey asked how much longer things should get worse before the citizens rise, warning that there may be a danger that in their self-confidence, they may allow their defense to get too far to the extent that an easy cure may not be possible. He believed that there were times a revolution was needed as the only remedy. In his words:

"There comes a time when the only remedy is a revolution. Can we be sure that our virtues are so remarkable, our situation so peculiar, our strength so great that the fate which has befallen other republics can by no accident be ours? Such are the questions that disturb our repose."

Storey did not end his address without proposing remedies to the issues he had talked about in his speech. He believed that when it came to the legislature, no system of government could be successful unless those in charge were men of ability and integrity. According to him, "The challenge is that we have failed to choose our officers; instead, we have allowed them to choose themselves."

Each vote needs to be assured of its proper influence on the election results. Once that is achieved, the next thing to do (to secure an appropriate legislature) is to ensure that each voter expresses their opinion unintimidated, "unbribed," and that the results are finally declared with all honesty. According to Storey, if they were to purify the legislature, it was crucial first to refine the campaign and ensure abolishing the prolific source of direct bribery: the campaign fund, which is the convenient cover for the indirect purchase of the Legislature.

Storey believed that the vast sums of money collected were spent to indirectly demoralize the voters and purchase executive and legislative office – though this was not even the worst use of the campaign funds. He, therefore, proposed the use of the English system, which he thought was a more efficient way to stop the enormous expenditure that was being tolerated. The English system frowns at the improper payment made by a candidate or, in a bid to protect his interest, unseats any candidate that is found to violate this law. In worst cases, the corrupted constituency will be disfranchised. He agreed that it was the right decision to separate the national, state, and municipal elections, and the referendum may become necessary considering the increasing complexity of political life.[18]

Storey focused his attention on several causes that he firmly believed in during his career. He spoke against lynching, which was rampant and affecting African Americans who were innocent in some cases. In his address at the opening of Petrigru College, he understood that one primary reason lynching continued unabated was because of delays or failures of the law. He knew that it was only natural that as children witnessed these barbaric acts, they would end up learning from their parents, and he was concerned that when they eventually came of age to govern the country, they may also do the same thing or even worse. The only way to stop this vicious circle was to stop the issue of lynching by addressing such cases properly.

It was evident that the weak and lowly in society were the ones who suffered the consequences of condoning lawlessness. Still, Storey was concerned that the rate of violence would increase if citizens failed to get justice and enjoy equal opportunity. He had his strong views regarding politicians who, in his opinion, did not fulfill the promises they made. Although he supported several politicians on different issues, he firmly believed that in terms of civil service reform, honest money, tariff reform, and honest election, no party was to be trusted.

Moorfield Storey and the Mugwumps (1896)

The National Democratic Party (NDP) came into existence in 1896 and was formed by leading advocates of classical liberalism in the late nineteenth century. However, a few founding members were already aware of the fate of their new party and the philosophy of limited government it promoted. Learning about the NDP will help better understand the decline of classical liberalism and the emergence of modern liberalism. Those who founded the NDP were mainly disenchanted democrats who were focused on preserving the ideals of Grover Cleveland and Thomas Jefferson. For over a century, the democrats had always held the strong belief:

> *"In the ability of every individual, unassisted, if unfettered by law, to achieve his own happiness and had upheld his right and opportunity peaceably to pursue whatever course of conduct he would, provided such conduct deprived no other individual of the equal enjoyment of the same right and opportunity."*

They have always stood for freedom of speech, freedom of trade, freedom of contract, and freedom of conscience – all of these are offshoots of the century-old battle cry of the party, which is "*Individual Liberty.*" Several classical liberals, such as E.L. Godkin, the editor, and publisher of the Nation,[19] President Cleveland,[20] and others, gave the NDP their support.

The NDP's origin can be linked to broader shifts in political alignments between 1876 and 1896 as the Democratic and Republican parties vied in almost complete equilibrium. At the time, electoral margins were extremely thin, and there was about 80 percent turnout of eligible voters; it was rare to find ticket-splitting. What often determined victory then was getting the party faithful to the polls on election day.[21,22,23]

The two most contentious issues were the gold standard and the tariff. After the increased popularity of Cleveland in the 1880s, the Democrats were in full support of free trade and hard money.[22] They fought liquor prohibition and Sunday blue laws at the local and state levels. The Republicans favored a more interventionist agenda of protective tariffs, legislation to regulate morals, and less focus on monetary inflation.[22,23,24]

Unfortunately, the country started experiencing a major economic depression, which Cleveland blamed on the moderate inflationist Sherman Silver Purchase Act of 1890. The Act was enacted under the previous Republican administration, and it required the Department of the Treasury to buy 4.5 million ounces of silver each month. Being afraid of abandonment of the gold standard, foreigners and Americans rushed to exchange dollars for gold. However, Cleveland pressed for the Silver Purchase Act to be repealed to restore financial confidence. His campaign was quite successful, but it could not reverse the drain immediately because it was painfully slow.[25,26,27]

Also, among those who strongly supported the NDP were members of the popular mugwumps – a group of self-described "independent voters" who were known for upholding principle over party.[28] The majority of the mugwumps were college-educated individuals living in northeastern states, like Massachusetts, and were of distinguished Yankee ancestry. Many of them worked in academia, journalism, and law.[29] One mugwump who strongly supported the NDP was Storey. Being involved in the fight against slavery had also become a defining life experience of the older mugwumps. For instance, the mugwumps had identified themselves with Lincoln and supported the Union cause.

They had also raised funds to assist in equipping John Brown's insurgent army in Kansas.[30,31] The younger mugwumps, like Storey, usually had personal or family ties to the anti-slavery movement. For instance, Storey had been Senator Charles Sumner's secretary. The mugwumps left the Republican party in disgust over the level of corruption of the Grant administration. They gradually became close to the Democratic party and were satisfied with Cleveland advocating civil service reform, free trade, and a gold standard.[28] The mugwumps obtained their free-market views from several sources, like Harriet Martineau, Adam Smith, and Herbert Spencer.[32]

Although the NDP was encouraged by its strong showing in some congressional races, the new party faced several disappointments. The party's hopes were significantly dashed by its weak performance in the 1897 and 1898 elections. There were increased hopes for the party's renewal with the rise of the American Anti-Imperialist League after the Spanish-American War. The league's purpose, which was established in November 1898, was to challenge the annexation of the Philippines and other captured territories.

Many anti-imperialists started making plans to combine forces with the NDP and launch a third presidential ticket in 1900. Initially, the chances of establishing such an alliance appeared quite promising. Storey was a vice president of the league and later became its president; Edwin Burritt Smith was the chair of its executive committee.[33] Unfortunately, the plan for a third ticket did not work out despite the efforts of Storey, Osborne, Villard, Morton, and others.

It became increasingly evident as the election got closer that Bryan had managed to handle the issue of anti-imperialism effectively, and the individuals who desired a third-party bid were few. Also, the gold standard appeared to be certain under McKinley. Consequently, in 1900, as its last official act, the national committee of the NDP agreed that nomination of a third ticket "for the offices of President and Vice President is unwise and inexpedient."[34]

Nothing to Excuse Our Intervention (1898)

As earlier mentioned, Storey was strongly against the U.S. going to war, and this is not a surprise since his views might have been encouraged by his association with Charles Sumner. But one of the addresses made by Storey, which depicts his opinion about the U.S. going to war against Spain and Cuba, was the one he gave during the meeting of the Massachusetts Reform Club on April 8, 1898. He expressed his concerns that the circumstances under which the members met perhaps caused the highest level of anxiety to every patriotic man in the United States.

To Moorfield, a patriotic man does not mean an individual who measures the greatness of his country by the extent of her territory, the strength of her fleets, the size of her armies or the impudence with which the country crushes her weaker neighbors. Instead, it is an individual who understand that the true greatness of a man – and also a nation – depends on their sense of justice, magnanimity, character and self-restraint. He decried the fact that even after nineteen centuries, the United States, though it had boasted to be a part of the civilization at the time, had abandoned the policy of peace with all mankind.

Unfortunately, this was what was adopted during the formation of the government and was the reason the country became great. He believed they forsook the nation's real leaders – such as the president, the speaker of the house, and experienced veterans of the Senate – and surrendered their conscience and heart to what he called "irresponsible mercenaries like the conductors of the World, the New York Journal, and other individuals who are calling for war for different motives."

In Storey's opinion, war was simply the worst of human calamities and hardly affected the guilty who caused the war in the first place. He firmly believed that war often destroys the innocent and overwhelms men, women, and children with underserved misfortune since they are not responsible for the same evils that the war aims to resolve. To support his views, he quoted the words of one of the great generals of the United States regarding war ("war is hell") and added the remarks of Sidney Smith, that, "In war, God is forgotten."

In his address, he wondered why the nation was suddenly faced with the frightful disaster of going to war with Spain, which would not only lead to the fearful loss of life and destruction of property but would affect an orderly government, lead to national hatred, demoralize the people, increase widespread corruption, and eventually lead to a return of barbarous standards, all part of what war causes. So, with the possibility of such terrible outcomes, Storey asked his audience why the U.S. was trying to turn back the tide of civilization.

He agreed that many forces were influencing the war with Spain. Specifically, he mentioned the interests represented in high federal offices, where some individuals believed that the war would improve business and make the rich wealthier. To buttress his point, he quoted the reply made by someone he described as "a Middlesex Yankee of pure blood." According to the man, who happened to be a manufacturer and dealer of woolen goods; *We want war. Just think how it will raise the price of wool, and how it will send your goods up."*

The war would indeed increase the price of wool and goods, but Storey quickly educated his audience on the cost of the war. There was no better way to express his irritation about becoming wealthy courtesy of the war than his exact words:

> *"I can't afford to dye my goods in American blood. It comes too high. The man who will send others – husbands, fathers, sons, brothers – to die, in order that his gains may be greater, must be counted with the wretches who visit the battlefield to plunder the slain."*

He believed that politicians in support of the war to influence their political ambition positively belong to the same class since they see men as counters who may be injured or killed to ensure they retain their position in politics. In Storey's opinion, journalists who see the war to increase the circulation of their media and daily sales, regardless of how others suffer, also belong to the same class.

The group of individuals who clamored for war and who Storey believed should be treated with respect were those who thought that humanity requires the intervention of the United States in Cuba. He believed these men (mainly ministers of God, philanthropists, and individuals of good conscience) were inflamed by the tales of suffering in Cuba, which they read every day in the daily newspapers until they concluded that going to war to end such inhumane conditions was a duty.

Although he believed these individuals should be treated kindly for their decision to support the war, Storey thought war should not be an option until all efforts to prevent it had failed. He believed that it was only when it became apparent that the evils the war would cure exceeded the evils it would cause could war become the only option. But he asked if the war with Spain was necessary and if it would do the nation any good.

In his judgment, the situation in Cuba did not excuse the intervention of the United States, and he believed that every consideration of patriotism and humanity was against the war because it would increase every evil in Cuba and the United States without correcting any evil. Storey concluded by saying, "If we are, as we pretend to be, a civilized and Christian people, let us insist that there be no war."[35]

Older mugwumps fought against slavery even before the younger ones, like Storey, got involved in the fight. They valued principle over party, which is one reason they decided to set up a new party that aligned with their ideologies. Perhaps the factors that inspired Storey to become highly involved in the new political party were the culmination of the challenges in governance, a corrupt legislature, and policies that he did not support.

Storey's opinion regarding the war in Spain and Cuba can be found in his definition of a patriotic man. He believed that a patriotic man understands that man's true greatness is based on his sense of magnanimity, self-restraint, character, and a sense of justice. He saw the war with Spain and Cuba as unnecessary and an event that would only affect the innocent. What worried him the most was the belief that the war with Spain would yield economic gains to the wealthy and positively influence the political ambition of politicians who supported it. It was evident that the only way he could have supported the war with Spain and Cuba would be after all attempts to prevent it had failed.

Storey's Biography of Charles Sumner (1900)

Storey was in an excellent position to write a biography of Charles Sumner. His association with Sumner offered him the chance to understand who Sumner was. In his biography, he boldly declared that in case a monument for individuals who were unconscious benefactors of the Republic was erected, the name of the man who refused cadetship to Charles Sumner (who was just fifteen years at the time) should be among the names inscribed upon such a monument. This is quite an interesting and amusing way to describe someone. But why did Storey make such a remark? The answer lies in the qualities of Charles Sumner – reticence, courage, patience, and other attributes that every perfect soldier possessed. Storey also did not fail to add that the great Senator lacked strategy.

According to Story's detailed genealogy of Charles Sumner, he was of purely English descent. His ancestors from both sides moved to the colonies about two centuries before Sumner was born. Sumner, a Bostonian and Harvard graduate, was the son of Job Sumner, also a Harvard student. According to history records, his father dropped his books when he heard the shots at Lexington and fought at Bunker Hill. He later became second in command of the force that guarded New York during the British evacuation.

Charles Sumner was a member of the class of 1830, and because he never liked mathematics and physics, he focused more of his time and efforts on literature, history, and the classics. He did not make efforts to take high honors; when he finally graduated, he taught school for some weeks. When he eventually decided to enter Law School, his ambitions were awakened, and he began to study hard. Although he made friends everywhere, he was among the few students who became friends with Judge Joseph Story. One year after his graduation, Charles Sumner's visit to Washington brought him honors and attention.

Storey recounts that the country was still small in those days, so it was easy to identify a promising young man of only twenty-three years.

Despite the attention, Sumner refused to be influenced negatively, and his state of mind was expressed in a letter which he wrote to his father shortly after hearing the Congressional debates regarding the U.S. Bank matter:

"I probably shall never come here again. I have little or no desire ever to come again in any capacity. Nothing that I have seen of politics has made me look upon them with any feeling other than loathing. The more I see of them the more I love law, which I feel will give me an honorable livelihood."

Sumner spent three years practicing, studying, and teaching in law school. This also broadened his familiarity with the best men of his time. Although his eloquence and oration made him a leader among his compatriots, it also made him some enemies due to his complete lack of empathy. His unkind remarks on volunteer uniforms and two of his questions especially displeased those from the navy yards and the other forts: *"What use is the army of the United States? What use is the navy of the United States?"* Although his real life started when he was nearly thirty-five years, the preparation for it had been a long and thorough one. According to Storey, Sumner was a scholar, an orator, and a gentleman who was adequately equipped to represent his countrymen's best thoughts and feelings.

He joined the Senate without the customary preliminary sessions in the House. In his first speech, he argued against intervention in foreign politics but was silent on the slavery question for five months while getting accustomed to his new position and surroundings. As soon as Sumner was prepared for work, he became irritating and denunciatory to his opponents, more so than any other individual who has ever addressed the Senate chamber. Records from the House reveal the extent to which his speeches possessed such characteristics. In Storey's view, the manner of Sumner's speech was excellent. Still, the superficial civility and rhetoric did not in any way console individuals who were regarded as robbers, liars, and oppressors.

One natural but unjustified effect of Sumner's words was Brook's assault. However, perhaps the most pathetic spectacle in American political life (except for those afforded by the death of its two martyrs) was the effort of the strong man to carry out his duties while suffering and his decision to hold on to his office so as not to miss his chance to defend righteousness. Sumner's opponents found him more robust than ever when he returned to his seat in 1859 because his presence in the House was a rebuke to the slaveholder and, at the same time, a boost to the Republicans.

Storey pointed out it was easy to wish that Sumner had a little more imagination and humor; however, the toleration provided by most of these qualities often extends to their possessor's faults as well as sins. In his view, men with similar attributes like Sumner must be somewhat intolerant. In 1840, Sumner was quite political while delivering the Phi Beta Kappa oration, disguising his attacks on war and slavery as a eulogy on Story, Pickering, William Ellery Channing, and Aliston. He managed to express his opinion without offending others and even went ahead to please judges with tastes as diverse as Emerson's and Everett's.

It is interesting to note that Storey attributed emancipation and equal rights for the African American to Sumner more than other individuals in the United States, except Lincoln. He also attributes the prevention of war with France and England to Sumner more than any other individual. However, those familiar with Mr. Adam's diplomatic work may not agree with him. According to Charles Sumner's theory in his *Prophetic Voices,* perpetual peace would gradually draw other countries on the continent, including South America, to the United States. Storey's biography of Sumner was delivered in style and combined with his sympathetic admiration of Sumner. He was not afraid to mention his faults or shortcomings as a human being and did not fail to showcase his excellent qualities.[36]

Speech at The Centenary of the Birth of Emerson (1903)

An event organized by Concord's leading men's club, known as the Social Circle, included Ralph Waldo Emerson as a member of the club. The event was organized to celebrate the centenary of Emerson's birth.

Storey honored Emerson for teaching him what he called the "most valuable lessons" about human dignity:

"That every man, ... white, brown, or black had his right to his chance of success, and it followed that no other man had a right to take that chance."

The lessons Storey learned from Emerson influenced him beyond what Emerson could have ever imagined.

Storey had access to Emerson's famous "lost journal", since he could borrow from the Emerson family library for the presentation. The notebook was called *Liberty*, and it contained his notes on abolition and slavery. It was eventually lost in Storey's papers, since he did not return it to the family. Interestingly, the revealing manuscript was later found in 1964 after being deposited alongside other books in the Library of Congress.

Storey's closeness to the Emerson family was a primary reason he was invited to give a speech during the Emerson Centenary. He did not show how immensely Ralph Waldo Emerson influenced him during his speech. He started his speech by first mentioning that there was really nothing he would say that was not already known by Emerson's friends. Storey believed he had a sense of personal obligation to Emerson for the lessons Emerson taught him and was challenged by the invitation to give a speech to share his experiences, which he saw as a debt. He did not speak as a contemporary or an equal, having been the friend of Emerson's son Edward.

Instead, Storey mentioned that he was speaking as someone who represented the younger generation that the words of Emerson had profoundly influenced. One of the experiences he shared was about the evening he encountered Emerson, meeting him for the first time in the early days of his college course. He recalled Emerson's gracious simplicity of manner at his table. He described Emerson's demeanor as that of a learner who often portrayed the attitude of someone who believes the ideas of his visitor would be of interest to him.

Storey believed most of the lessons he learned while in college were from the writings of Ralph Waldo Emerson. One of these lessons, which he also talked about during his speech, is that the moral laws of the universe are as inexorable as the physical laws governing our solar system – they all execute themselves.

> *"There exists in the soul of man a justice that comes with instant and complete retributions. So, all those who do good are immediately ennobled while those who engage in evil deeds are by their actions contracted. So, theft can never enrich a person and arms can never make someone impoverished."*[37]

Edward Waldo Emerson Speech (1903)

Edward's speech started with fond family recollections of one of the remarks his father often made, which his mother also imbibed – "Ten years ago today, such a thing happened." Other members of the family would also take turns recalling other anniversaries. He recalled that Emerson would often laugh when he made such remarks while they were at the table, such as, "Oh, it is always a hundred years from something."

While remembering the fire incident that affected his father's house, he believed that some of those present were too young to recall the incident. But he highlighted Emerson's friends' historic courage and efforts, some of whom were present at the event, who risked their lives to prevent the fire from destroying his father's properties and even saved all his effects.

After the fire incident, Emerson's friends sent him abroad to receive medical attention. When it was time for him to come home, news of his return spread, and his friends were told that the engineer would toot the whistle while the train went down the grade from Walden Woods to indicate that Emerson was on board. Those who gathered to welcome Emerson carried him home happily, and friends and neighbors surrounded him while school children marched alongside. However, he added that his father had thought in good faith that all the jubilation and celebration was a tribute to Ellen, his sister, but did not know it was meant for him.

After he passed through the triumphal arch and got to his door, he found his home just as he had left it. There were no traces of the fire incident or destruction that took place. His study was as before the fire, and all his books were accounted for. Emerson also saw many of his friends and neighbors surrounding his gate. At that point, it dawned on him that the celebration was all about his return. Edward admitted to his audience that he would not be able to say all that his father said at that moment, even though he uttered a few words, and this is because the meaning of what he said was found in the expression on his face.

In Emerson's words, *"My friends and neighbors! I am not wood nor stone."* Although his words were few, the meaning was clear, and many understood it. Edward tried to explain why people felt the way they did regarding Emerson. He was not born in Concord and always followed his own lines, regardless of other people's ideas. He was a scholar who lived apart. He believed these were among the reasons people initially regarded him as someone crazy, then atheistic, then pantheistic, then a mere mystic, and, finally, they accepted him.

But why did the people eventually accept him? There were two reasons for this acceptance, and one of them was that his father never fought. All he did was share his message, and he did not try to defend what he said. Emerson was of the view that the truth he believed would protect itself, and it needed no defense. Emerson left the words he spoke to work their way, and this was why he aroused no opposition.

People accepted him because he always found good in all things, even in the fierce wars of the Middle Ages, and was prepared to answer for his word with his life, which he did. He believed that even though a few people were reading his words while he was alive, his life was before them; all those who read his words realized how humble, sweet, expectant, hopeful, and serene his life was, and they became his friends.

Edward added that his father made friends the same way the sun in heaven makes friends. Emerson attended to his duty to his town, country, and globe. He attended town meetings even when he was discouraged by his neighbor on the hill not to attend. According to his neighbor, "What you do with the ballot is no use – it won't stay so; but what you do with the gun stays done." Emerson still attended the town meeting, and in his words:

> *"What business have you to stay away from the polls because you paired off with a man who means to vote wrong? How shall you, who mean to vote right, be excused from staying away? Suppose the three hundred Spartans at Thermopylae had paired off with an equal number of Persians. Would it have been the same to history? Would it have been the same to the world?"* [37]

No one was in a better position to write a biography of Charles Sumner than Storey, and a look at the biography shows he had a thorough and balanced understanding of who Sumner was. We can conclude that Storey regarded Sumner as a major actor in the fight for equal rights for Blacks in the United States. He gave a detailed explanation of the sacrifices, determination, and commitment of Sumner toward defending righteousness and rebuking slaveholders. It was Sumner's commitment to ensuring equal rights for African Americans that motivated him to maintain his seat despite the threats he faced at the time.

It is also clear that apart from Senator Sumner and his father, other persons like Ralph Waldo Emerson also played a key role in his life, as earlier noted in the first chapter. He admitted that even Emerson would be amazed to know how the lessons he learned from him influenced his life. His access to freely borrow books from Emerson's family library offered him the chance to read a good number of his personal books, including the famous lost journal. His invitation to give a speech during Emerson's Centenary proves how close he was to the family and perhaps his greatest takeaway from his association with Emerson was the moral laws of the universe.

Letters (1904-1912)

It seems that part of the reason Storey wrote this letter to George L. Fox was in response to his request made in a previous letter. This letter was written on February 2, 1904, and he started by first expressing how delighted he was to send twenty-five copies of his speech to Fox. Storey shed light on his theory of a citizen's duty, which is to use their lawful influence in settling general questions and doing everything possible to ensure they are adequately resolved. In his view, doing this implied that the citizen had performed their full duty and would be bound to do it without considering whether their efforts would be successful or not.

Storey reminded Fox that he would use the resultant forces as an illustration, just as he had always done before. In his view, every person was a force and would deflect the resistance if they pushed and, if not, it would be deflected against the person. So, no one is entitled to affect to any significant extent beyond what their force permits. Storey declared that it was crucial to make it clear that not all citizens of the U.S. accepted what he called "the Panama crime." In his view, the criticisms may not correct the wrong; however, speaking against such issues would ensure that people would find it extremely difficult to commit such types of crimes in the future. He described such criticism as a process of education that can strengthen people's opinions.[38]

One of Storey's letters was addressed to Charles E. Ward of the House of Representatives, Boston, and was written to accept heading the board members of one of the committees, which comprised a hundred advisers of the Jamestown Exhibition. While accepting the role, Storey used the occasion to address some of the questions in the previous letter dated March 29, 1906. As he admitted, providing an answer to the question was not an easy one.

In line with his strong beliefs, Storey expressed his views that every citizen's most crucial political duty was to do all in their power to secure for all American citizens equal political rights, equal standing before the law, and equal opportunity regardless of their race or color. This is in complete alignment with what he fought for in his lifetime. Storey added that this was also the duty of the State of Massachusetts and its legislature.

The main reason the committees were set up was in response to the invitation to be represented in the Jamestown Exhibition, even as the state was asked to allocate funds for the exhibition. The African Americans who had witnessed several cases of abuse of their rights at the time refused to be a part of the exhibition. Their reason for objecting was because they believed they were not going to be received at the exhibition on equal terms with whites. Storey further added that they refused to participate out of fear of being exposed to social discrimination.

While Storey acknowledged there were no threats to support what the African Americans feared, he explained that they objected to the event because their fear was based on what they already experienced of the common attitude of white men toward African Americans, especially in the Southern states. In his opinion, the refusal of an appropriation would be because the authorities of Jamestown Exhibition would allow such kind of discrimination.

He concluded by saying that if the committee was satisfied that the distinction between African Americans and white men of Massachusetts would be recognized by the authorities of the exhibition or State, then in his opinion, the legislature as trustees of a fund obtained from taxes imposed on all citizens should refrain from spending any of such funds for the exhibition. Storey made this statement because African Americans would be excluded from benefiting from such expenditure even when they paid tax. [39]

He was unable to attend the commemoration of Charles Sumner's birth. Still, he did not fail to offer his opinion on how the event should be organized, especially regarding racism. He addressed this letter to William M. Trotter on December 30, 1910. While wishing that the event was successful, he advised that the celebration needed to be promoted by an organization of colored Americans. According to Storey, their race owed much to Mr. Sumner, who devoted his life to working to secure for colored Americans not just emancipation but also equality of rights, both civil and political, which Mr. Sumner often regarded as "the first of rights."

Storey added that they equally owed him a great debt on the part of white men. In his opinion, Sumner was a leader in the movement that liberated white Americans from the burden and crime of enslaving their fellow men. According to Storey:

"It is not he who sustains but he who inflicts a wrong that suffers most thereby, and every person in this country is better and happier

today by reason of the labors and sacrifices of Charles Sumner and his associates."

He was strongly convinced that even though Sumner's long struggle was rewarded by victory, as he explained in his letter, the work he had at heart was still not finished and would not be complete until the prejudices of race and color were forgotten. He summarized his letter by declaring that the celebration of the birth of Mr. Sumner should help refresh memories of the battles he won while he was alive and further inspire people to persevere until the realization of Sumner's ideals. He added that the event should inspire them to resolve that for the sake of colored and white Americans alike, there should no longer be any form of inequality in the way American citizens were treated, which, in his opinion, was the root of bitterness and strife and could hinder the civilization of the United States.[44]

Storey's letter to Francis B. Sears, on May 6, 1911, was in respect of the setting up of a branch house at the south end by the Boston Young Men's Christian Association. The branch house was to be established for exclusive use by non-white members of the association. At the time, Sears was one of the Association's directors, and it is evident from the beginning that Storey was not happy with the development. He clearly expressed the hope that the project would not be successful.

In his view, people needed to avoid engaging in any action that may in some way be seen to promote or recognize the race prejudice, which he believed was hindering the progress of colored individuals in the United States. To justify his views, Storey referred to Baltimore's situation when they attempted to restrict the area where people of color could live, a trend that was also taking place in other locations in the U.S. To further bolster his point, he described the kind of experience that colored men were facing in the U.S. at the time. He also added that labor unions had not agreed to accept them but only permitted just their members to work while excluding non-members.

He recalled how he was informed previously that about 22,000 African Americans were almost deprived of the opportunity to work in Washington. These men were used as teamsters a few years prior, but the trend at the time of his letter had changed as masons had to stop working if colored teamsters delivered a load of stone at a building. In Storey's words, such acts were "so cruel, so mean and so unjust" that he hoped every good citizen of the United States, especially Christian organizations, would resist such trends.

In his letter, Storey spoke as one who understood how the African Americans felt regarding the establishment of the branch when he informed Sears that regardless of the motivation behind setting up the branch, colored men would regard it as segregation. He advised Sears that if the association had many members who required facilities in the south end, there was nothing wrong with granting their wish. Still, he added that there was no justification for excluding white members from the proposed building or in any way concluding that it was proper to set up a separate building for their colored members.

He disclosed that colored citizens of Boston had a powerful feeling in the matter, one he shared. He expressed his hope that the scheme would be abandoned, or he would be sorry that the association, which advocates the doctrine of Christianity, should engage in activities that would offer their enemies the opportunity to ridicule them.[40]

On April 22, 1912, Storey wrote a letter to Col. Hallowell. He began by acknowledging that he had previously received Hallowell's note sent on April 20, 1912. The reason for the letter was to talk about Roosevelt's action in Brownsville. He believed that Roosevelt's action was in no way influenced by racial prejudice. Storey strongly believed that Roosevelt did not consider the fact that he would get public attention by inviting Booker Washington to lunch just as he or Hallowell should have done.

He shared his belief that when Roosevelt discovered that he had lost support from the South by his action, he decided to recover by what he did in the Brownsville case. This was also what took place in Akron, Ohio, with a white regiment, and the way the War Department acted in the case was utterly protective, even though what happened occurred in broad daylight and there was no doubt that the white soldiers shot up the town. Shortly afterward, the Brownsville case emerged with a conspicuously arbitrary policy and differed entirely from what was previously done in the case of the white regiment and continued in it, even though its error was unraveled.[43]

Storey added that the president's course of action in the matter was entirely deceitful in at least one way and that single action served as the reason why Storey condemned him. He proceeded to talk about the president's action and how it displeased him greatly. According to Storey, the president failed to invite colored individuals to his table and even failed to take reasonable action on the issue of lynching, which was common at the time. This, in his view, was what was expected from the United States' President, especially one that freely expressed himself on all kinds of public questions. He ended his note by pointing out how he differed from Col. Hallowell in their assessment of Roosevelt. Storey regarded Roosevelt as completely unreliable; he regarded him as the most dangerous individual in public life.[43]

This letter was written to George Tucker on May 6, 1912. Storey was quick to express how delighted he was to have received Tucker's note on May 3, 1912. Tucker had expressed his appreciation for Storey's work, which explains why Storey disclosed that he was also glad that Tucker found his work interesting. He also revealed that even though his write-up was for young people, it also contained reflections of the old. Just like he did when he wrote to Hallowell, the focus of this letter was to talk about President Theodore Roosevelt. Storey informed Tucker that he was not the type to praise Roosevelt, and if Tucker needed someone to eulogize Roosevelt, who he described as an unscrupulous marplot, he should search for someone else.

Just as he had earlier mentioned in one of his letters, Storey regarded Roosevelt as the most dangerous individual that had ever been in politics as far as he could recall and added that he was still involved in the most mischievous task. According to Storey, if there was something he could do to defeat Roosevelt, he was prepared to do it, but he would vote the Democratic ticket and was not going to vote for Taft or any of his kind. Storey informed Tucker that the reason for Roosevelt's generous acts in Massachusetts was to increase his influence in other states, as he believed that by having the doctrine adopted (he had already taken advantage of this in Massachusetts), he would win the heart of more delegates than those he would lose in Massachusetts.

Storey concluded by stating that he did not trust Roosevelt's generosity. At the time of writing this letter, Storey anticipated traveling with his wife to Europe by the end of May 1912 and would stay abroad with her. It was apparent that their trip to Europe enabled his wife to get medical attention. He added that he could only return to the U.S. when his wife was ready, in early August. Storey explained in his letter that he would have greatly loved to visit Tucker, but he had a lot of things to do at the time.[41]

On December 19, 1912, Storey wrote a letter to Dr. Theodore Schott, who was in Germany, to inform him of the death of Mrs. Storey. It seemed that their journey to Europe, which he talked about in his letter to Tucker, was to meet with Prof. Schott. This also explains why Storey wrote to Schott informing him of the passing of his wife on November 27, 1912. While describing what happened, he explained that his wife had returned from Europe and appeared to be quite strong and full of spirits. Undoubtedly, Storey had enjoyed their journey because he described it as a pleasant one.

They had traveled through locations such as Normandy and Brittany during their trip before they finally sailed back to the United States. Prof. Schott had earlier sent a letter to Storey and his wife explaining her heart condition, which he described as satisfactory. This letter confirmed part of the reason why they had traveled to Europe. Schott's earlier letter reassured Storey that his wife's health was re-established, and she would enjoy more years. But this turned out not to happen. His wife suddenly started experiencing violent pain caused by issues with her intestine.

Several efforts were made to stop the pain, but the only option was to operate when medical efforts failed to resolve the health issue. The outcome of the operation revealed that his wife had a perforated ulcer in the upper region of her stomach, which had also led to peritonitis. The operation was successful, and he revealed that his wife recuperated without suffering any shock or disturbances of her heart. It seemed that before they traveled to Europe, his wife was already having issues with her heart.

After the operation, which was carried out on a Thursday, he explained that doctors had pronounced that his wife was out of danger on Saturday. She had continued to recover well after two or three days of the operation, but her pulse started to flutter on Wednesday at about 3:00 pm, and by 7:00 pm, she had died. He disclosed that what caused her death appeared to be a fragment of tissue that entered circulation and eventually resulted in something like an embolism. It is evident that doctors had done everything to stimulate the heart and revive her, but they failed to resuscitate her. It was indeed a painful experience for him, even as he revealed that he was fortunate to be consoled by his children, friends, and pleasant memories.[42]

Most of the letters written by Storey reflected his opinion regarding several issues. He always expressed his views regarding the duty of every U.S. citizen to ensure that all American citizens could enjoy equal political rights and equal opportunity in standing before the law, regardless of race or color. We can see this as a summary of what he fought for all his life, and he would often refer to it whenever he had the chance. He did not waste time frowning at attempts to create a distinction between white men and African Americans and would rather suggest that an occasion be canceled instead of holding it in a way that would foster segregation.

Regardless of the nature of the occasion – a church activity, an exhibition, etc. – he opposed actions that might in any way recognize or promote race prejudice as he firmly believed that the progress of African Americans was being hindered by it and it should be prevented. He was greatly bothered by race prejudice as he condemned it in strong terms as cruel, mean, and unjust. His letters focused on political events in the U.S., issues of equal rights, and the law. Of course, he did not fail to criticize politicians, and, in one of his letters, he referred to Roosevelt as the most dangerous person that has ever been in politics as far as he could remember. He also wrote about the loss of his wife. Indeed, he loved his wife and did all he could to save her by taking her to Europe for treatment. It appeared that the cause of her death was different from the main reason why they traveled.

SPEECHES

Not More Laws, but Reform of
Present Ones Needed (1912)

M EMBERS OF THE Council of the National Economic League, comprising 800 members from different sectors, interests, and opinions such as bankers, university presidents, merchants, and professors, were asked to choose topics from a list of subjects for public discussion. The ones they chose should be the topics they felt were the most important among the list of topics. The "direct legislation" question was top on their list, above questions like the tariff, labor troubles, and conservation. One of the questions they also added was "inefficiency and delay of the courts in the administration of justice."

Storey was given the task of pointing out ways to reform legal procedures without altering the law and further suggesting possible changes that would be beneficial when made. As a distinguished lawyer and a former President of the American Bar Association, the speech gave him the opportunity to talk about the state of the legal process in the United States, focusing on the present state of things. While delivering his speech, Storey contended that there were too many existing laws and a need to apply common sense in administering the available laws. He believed this would help remedy most of the ills the nation was suffering. Storey argued that the average citizen of the United States thought that the solution to any challenge they faced, no matter how small it may be, was the establishment of new laws, and he disagreed.

He felt this was why they were quick to fall back to the legislature with various kinds of proposals for legislation. Consequently, there would be a release of new laws upon the residents of every state annually or bi-annually. He firmly believed that any public-spirited citizen of the United States who witnessed the actions of the legislature and attempted to stop the foolish laws would be astonished by how the country was governed. Despite the increase in the number of laws being introduced into the country, Storey was of the view that there was no correspondent increase in the respect for the law; instead, the reverse was the order of the day – the more the laws in existence, the more available they were to break.

He was quick to identify that the popularity of the legal profession had dropped significantly, and, in his view, this was caused by lawyers. Although he had strong opinions about the law and reforms, Storey did not fail to remind the people that the reform process was not as easy as many had earlier thought. Although it is easy for everyone to embrace and praise progress in science, it was entirely a different matter regarding the progress made in law, political, or social life. However, the legal profession's leaders understood that there was a need to act.

One of the major complaints he described to be as old as the law itself had to do with delay. According to Storey, some level of delay was crucial to ensure justice. This is because there needed to be a proper investigation, and, in some cases, there is a need for more time for hot heads to cool. But what he frowned upon was prolonged delays, which he saw as unnecessary and could eventually lead to injustice.

He added that the oath taken by an attorney imposes on him a duty not just to his client but also his adversary. So, if the oath is appropriately applied, there would not be an issue of delay. He attributed the problem of delay in the law to the congestion of the dockets, and undoubtedly, if cases that ought not to be brought before the courts in the first place or those that should not be defended were eliminated, then the congestion would have been reduced drastically. According to Storey, the primary factor causing the delays – delays caused by the bringing of groundless suits and the making of false defenses – was low professional standards among lawyers or members of the Bar. The best way to solve the issue, in his opinion, was to create a public opinion that would not permit such practices or eliminate them via legislation.

Another way to stop this issue was to permit courts to fix the money that the losing party would have to pay. Theoretically, this cost was meant to cover all the expenses of the prevailing party that the opponent caused. However, in practice, such costs were insignificant. In his exact words, "If he who would thus abuse the law knew that he might be compelled to pay every dollar of expense to which he put his opponent, he would hesitate."

Storey disclosed that it would be a great idea if the court were given the permission or power to punish any lawyer who rendered their services to provide room for injustice. He suggested that one way to do this was to compel the lawyer to settle all the expenses that the opposing party incurred personally. He added that the English courts had already embraced a rule that allowed this kind of practice. While anticipating that there would be an objection that the standards he was setting were extremely high for the lawyer, he admitted that it was very likely that the standards were indeed too high. But he quickly added that the reason he was making such suggestions was to explain why the Bar was fast becoming less popular with the public and that one possible reason for this was the fact that the existing standards of practice were too low.

In Storey's opinion, the second reason for the delay in law was the imperfect nature of human beings. He described a trial as a long strain, and a specific belief often possesses those involved until a verdict was given; the individual gets a defeat that was seen as unmerited. However, a delay was often obtained in one way or another and this, he believed, was a severe evil. He cited an example of a man who told him that his former partner owed him $150,000 and had refused to pay the money. The suit for the settlement of the man's account had been pending for six years.

The delay was linked to the busy lawyers who were often not present at the same time, which resulted in a hearing for two or three days out of a year for the trial of the case. During this period, the man was growing older without his money and unable to solve his problem. Storey disclosed that he rejected the man's request to take up the case because he already had a capable counsel and nothing he could add to the case. Storey shared this story to explain why the public complained about the law's delay.

He further decried the increase in the number of cases brought to the courts alongside the delay on the part of the lawyers. To solve the issue, he suggested proper legislation to help remove the great cause of litigation, stating that the reason lawyers no longer dealt with disputes about insurance policies and real estate, which were the major disputes several years prior, was because of proper legislation. He explained that the courts were already being choked by actions for personal damages that had increased beyond proportion and further worsened by the increase in population.

He described the prosecution of such cases as a business that degraded the medical and legal professions. What Storey believed would solve the issue was partly based on systems that were popular in other countries, having to do with legislation that might eliminate such litigations. He suggested that the judge promptly avoid wasting time in asking unnecessary questions and wrangling between counsel. He described the examination of a witness by a lawyer as a sport where the lawyer got to enjoy himself, which eventually led to an unnecessary waste of time and delays.

To buttress his point, Storey gave an example of what he saw as an excellent strategy based on a tale from England where a judge refused to allow the council to call a witness and made the entire process fast. He described the case as making practical sense, adding that it would be a great idea to encourage consultation by the jurors under the supervision of the judge and counsel. He felt that this would foster attention to business and prevent the waste of time in the jury room. He further pointed out that trials should be carried out to ensure there would not be a need for a second trial of the same facts. To achieve this, he suggested adopting a practice that had already been repeatedly recommended by the American Bar Association, involving the submission of distinct issues of fact to the jury or requesting that they answer specific questions.

Storey's opinion regarding how to handle evidence was that the appellate court should be granted liberal discretion to sustain the verdict in situations where it was reasonably clear that the excluded or admitted evidence would not have changed the jury's conclusion or that the court's judgment was just. While bearing in mind that the trial judge could set aside an improper verdict and that it was pretty rare for the case to reach the appellate court until the power had been invoked, Storey recommended that the slight possibility of injustice as a result of a mistake made when dealing with evidence – which was often committed both by the trial judge as well as the appellate court – was nothing compared to the kind of injustice caused by the existing practice. This was also in addition to the delay and the expenses that both litigants and all parties in the same court were made to face because of repeated trials.

Storey argued that the power of appeal was, in some cases, a significant burden. For instance, a brakeman injured in 1882 only managed to recover damages after twenty-two years. The brakeman only received $6,500 under the New York system, which gave two appeals from the trial court – one to the court of appeal and one to the appellate division. During the trial, the brakeman changed his testimony several times; according to the court of appeal, the man changed his testimony in every trial. At this point, Storey lamented the poor situation of the judiciary, saying, "Oh justice, justice, what crimes are committed in thy name."

He cited other examples of cases that showcased the issues the judiciary was facing. Considering the problems he raised, Storey was convinced beyond doubt that there was a need to increase the power of the judge to enable them to influence the results in lower courts as in higher courts. He felt that the tendency of states to reduce the influence of the judge and add a slight increase in the jury's power, like that of skillful advocates, upon the result of the trial was completely wrong. He described the unwillingness to allow the judge to charge the jury on facts as absurd since the judge must decide the facts himself, even in the most complicated and crucial cases.

Using the case of a suit to dissolve the Standard Oil Trust as an example, Storey explained that in patent cases involving millions of dollars, the judge or lawyer appointed by the judge to act as master often determined the facts. But he felt this was ridiculous. In a case where a judge is sitting alone and possesses such powers, the judge was still forbidden to assist in determining a question of fact in the pettiest case, even when the judge possessed a stenographic record which the jury would rely on. In Storey's opinion, stenographic records were supposed to be sent to the jury whenever the judge believed it necessary.

However, whether this took place or not, Storey recommended that – just as it was being practiced in England at the time – the judge should refer to the question and discuss the evidence in his summing up. He believed that new judges who could be trusted should be chosen, especially when they couldn't trust their existing Judges. All these, in his opinion, were unnecessary delays before giving the first decision, along with the long delays in the higher courts.

Storey recommended a new rule: there should be an appeal to a bench of judges from the trial court, but this should be restricted to just one appeal. If the courts can't settle the case, a bench of lawyers should then settle it. In his opinion, it would be a better idea to have this kind of court instead of establishing an inferior court that would eventually make mistakes that a suitable court would later correct. Backing up his suggestions, he referred to the English Court of Appeals, which grants an average of twelve new trials annually, strictly based on merits. In his opinion, for his suggestions to be effective, there was a need to have good judges as he emphasized the importance of cheap justice.

Storey was convinced that those who have the resources to pay for the services of the best lawyers in the United States were great corporations, wealthy individuals, or the most dangerous criminals. It was the court's duty to stand between the community and the unjust claims of such individuals. While wondering how good judges could be obtained, he firmly believed that the public needed good lawyers, just as any private interest, and should also have the necessary funds required to hire their services. He went ahead to describe the existing conditions for the position of a judge in the United States.

Under the existing conditions, the position required a man of independent means or an individual whose professional success had been limited; however, taking up this position by a successful lawyer comes with a significant sacrifice. His experience as a committee member that searched for individuals who were qualified to fill the position and were willing to accept a seat on the bench informed his opinion regarding the issue. He narrated how several persons the committee members believed were qualified turned down the offer for various reasons.

Some felt that they needed to save their wife and kids and would not carry out their duty and live a comfortable life without making changes to their methods. For others, they did not like the idea of giving up their freedom. A few men felt capable and willing to take up the position based on duty and sacrifice, generally understood by everyone in the committee. This also explained why judges are appointed for life; reappointing judges regularly would make it difficult to secure good judges.

Storey lamented the difficulty in entering the bench as the candidates were often compelled to seek and pay for election at the hands of people. He felt that this made the tenure of the judge uncertain. In his opinion, limiting the powers of the judge in several ways was an indication of a lack of trust for the judges, and the challenges of the judges would be even further increased by what Storey regarded as "grossly inadequate salary." In his words:

> *"We are a businesspeople; we know that in private life, we could not get a good foreman on these terms, and we wonder that our courts are choked and the administration of the law expensive and uncertain. What common sense."*

He referred to billions of dollars appropriated for the United States' annual expenses during his speech. Seventy-two percent of the funds were spent on war, past, and future, compared to the meager amount allocated for the federal courts. In his opinion, the nation was giving millions of dollars for a force that they hoped never to use while leaving a few thousand for justice that was required daily in society, adding, "I hardly know which costs U.S. most, the expensive battleships or the cheap courts." While sharing some of his suggestions on remedies that could be applied to the judiciary system, including better courts with more extraordinary powers, Storey also discussed the things that could not be regarded as the remedy to the challenges.

Comparing the judiciary system in England with that of Massachusetts, Storey observed that while England was about twelve times as large as Massachusetts, it had only ninety-three judges compared to one hundred forty-four judges in Massachusetts. Citing other facts regarding the judiciary, he declared that what the country needed was not more judges and that this did not imply that more judges would reduce the issue of delay. He strongly felt that what mattered was not the number of judges but the quality of judges. He decried the failure of the courts to convict criminals despite the increased number of both judges and courts.

For instance, Storey pointed out that between 1887 and 1908, the total number of homicides committed in the U.S. rose from 1,200 to about 9,000. A total of forty-seven homicides were recorded on August 1, 1909, in Louisville, Kentucky, and there was no single execution. On the other hand, in London, which has a significant population, the total number of murder cases was nineteen and, out of this number, one of them died while awaiting trial, four were discovered to be insane, one killed himself in jail, four committed suicide, and four were executed. In his exact words, while describing how the law was being administered during his time:

> "The law as administered to-day, throws around the criminal a protecting wall which may have been necessary when the power of the English Crown pressed despotically on the subject, but which is wholly unnecessary today. It is the community that now needs protection from the criminal, not the innocent man who must be saved from injustice."

To give a clear picture of the state of the American courts during his time, Storey cited the case of a man convicted of murder in the first degree, but the verdict was set aside because the foreman misspelled "first" as "fist." In another instance, "breast" was spelled without an *a,* so the convicted murderer was given a new trial. He lamented the situation of things stating, "If we cannot alter the law so as to make such mockeries of justice impossible, our profession deserves the contempt of the community." He recommended that one way to stop the increasing corruption cases in the United States was for the law to desist from protecting the criminal and break down the shield of silence behind which the criminal hid from justice.

In summarizing, Storey referred to the ruling by the Supreme Court of the United States that, "under a statute properly drawn to protect him from prosecution and punishment, a man may be compelled to give evidence even though it criminates himself."

He suggested that they could at least pass statutes that extended this specific rule to other cases, like bribery, and possibly convict about half of the existing criminals at the expense of allowing the other half to go free, adding that "half a loaf is better than no bread." But he wondered why a sensible community should allow half of its most dangerous enemies to go free. He marveled at how they considered with much equanimity the prospects of losing thousands of innocent men in war but shuddered at the thought of asking a guilty man the right questions to discern his guilt. In his view, the Bar was responsible for the level of disrepute the legal profession found itself at the time. Storey believed that the seed of reform was available, and what would make more impact was the application of common sense and not the increased number of courts and laws.[45]

Storey's Presentation at Concord (1914)

On May 23, 1914, Storey delivered a speech at the unveiling of Ralph Waldo Emerson's statue in Concord which, in the words of Sanborn, is a town known for its "opposition to human slavery." Storey had been a friend of the Emerson family and, during a presentation given by Storey, his friendship with them provided him with sufficient information to describe Ralph Waldo Emerson and his thoughts on the issue of human rights, slavery, and abolition.

Storey was not only a longtime friend of the Emerson family; he was a classmate of Edward at Harvard and collaborated with him on a biography of Ebenezer Rockwood Hoar of Concord. During his presentation, Storey talked about various aspects of Ralph Waldo Emerson's thoughts on the need to assert human rights and abolish slavery. Part of Storey's address also focused on the methodology Emerson applied in attaining these goals, supporting his points with some of Emerson's journal.

During his presentation, Storey's explanation about how committed Emerson was to the basic integrity of every individual, as well as his unrelenting efforts to challenge all attempts to enslave and exploit others, was connected to his concern with some of the contemporary problems in the United States, such as racism.

Therefore, Storey further mentioned that Emerson was hopeful that some of the qualities that resulted in the exploitation of the Negro race during the nineteenth century, such as docility, industriousness, and benevolence, would not just defend U.S. independence in a more moral age, but would also offer them a rank among nations. But Storey remained convinced that, even in the twentieth century, the United States was not making any move toward the accomplishment of this dream, and he remarked:

> "How full of inspiration are these words to every lover of freedom and justice! How ineffably sad it is to read them now and to reflect as we listen to the cries of the mob at Wilmington and Evansville and read of the horrors committed in Luzon that ours is a less moral age and that punishment waits upon our sins as it did of our fathers."

Storey's closeness to the Emerson family helped create this presentation. His address was highly successful in highlighting Emerson's strong commitment toward the abolition cause and his firm belief in the sacredness of natural and individual rights. According to Franklin Sanborn, Storey's presentation shed significant light on the public's understanding of who Emerson was. Storey had the privilege of gaining access to Emerson's private journals and was free to quote from them. This enabled him to rehearse most of his popular opinions.[37]

The Negro's Fatherland (1917)

This piece was written by W.E.B. Du Bois in October 1917 while serving as the NAACP's Director of Publication and Research. Storey was serving as the organization's first President. The publication focused mainly on discussing Africa's future when World War I eventually ended. According to Du Bois, one of the most crucial questions to answer after the war was regarding the future of Africa. In his opinion, what further emphasized the importance of the question was the silence regarding the topic on both sides of the war. He noted that the enormous raw materials the modern world required were found in Africa more than on other continents. Africa also possessed the greatest world mine of undeveloped human labor. Some of the raw materials found in Africa included cocoa, diamonds, palm oil, lead, ebony, zinc, mahogany, copper, gold, tin, ostrich feathers, rubber, iron, cork, cotton, and ivory.

Those raw materials, in Du Bois' opinion, were Africa's gift to the world, while many other raw materials remained untapped. The primary cause of the war at the time was the fight for the ownership of these materials and the fight for who dominated the undeveloped labor. If this were the case, then there would undoubtedly be more wars in the future if the question regarding Africa was not resolved even after the war. So, he wondered why everyone was silent regarding the fate of between 150-200 million human beings. He presumed that the indifference was mainly psychological and the result of human degradation that usually exacts payment from the oppressor and oppressed. According to Du Bois, the Africans were being ignored at the time due to a history of degradation. The African blood was predominant in ancient Mediterranean civilizations and was present in almost all. The civilization and genius of Blacks are a great gift to the world.

African culture filtered into Europe in the European middle age. Legend, story, and song emerged from the "dark continent," though Africa was somehow separated from direct contact with Europe. There was no issue of racial inferiority based on skin color at the time. Unfortunately, toward the end of the fifteenth century, the African continent was raped by the world for four hundred years, to the extent that had never been seen before in human history. The outcome was the degradation of Africa and the moral degradation of those who carried out such inhumane acts.

Several decades after the invasion of Africa, the world still existed in the shadow of the debauch of the African slave trade. It was natural for many individuals who are never thought to live and view society as one established based on an "unsocial mudsill." [46] He further added that it was even possible for great labor organizations such as the American Federation of Labor to organize themselves based purely on aristocratic lines without considering individuals regarded as lower elements of labor. He felt it was also possible for an organization such as the League of Small and Subject Nationalities to only consider Africa accidentally as an after-thought. In Du Bois' words, "The mental attitude toward Africa and its problems builds itself upon unclear thinking based on the tyranny of conventional words."

People often think of modern African slavery as survival of ancient slavery, but that is incorrect because there is a remarkable difference between the two. Unlike ancient slavery, modern African slavery was the beginning of modern labor challenges. It is crucial to view and interpret it from that perspective; otherwise, we may get lost in an incorrect analogy. Modern imperialism, current labor issues, modern world commerce, and the modern factory system started with the African slave trade.

The first modern strategy for getting labor on a large or commercial scale (and mainly for gains) began in the middle of the fifteenth century with commerce between America and Africa. Africa lost a minimum of 100 million people through the slave trade, including the associated misery, economic issues, and social disorganization. Those who managed to survive this massive rape were turned into an international laboring force in the United States, leading to the establishment of the modern capitalist movement and the labor issues that emerged.

Ever since the enslavement of Blacks, efforts have been made to ensure that these Blacks and their descendants remain at the bottom of the scale since they were not complete men and could never become self-respecting members or contributors to modern culture. In Du

Bois' opinion, this assumption is strictly modern and undreamed of in both ancient and medieval days.

What could people expect if this same psychology and the efforts to exploit and continuously enslave people were being transferred to the new world after the war? Du Bois firmly believed that no modern world could ever hold 200 million individuals in permanent slavery, even if they were people of color. The price of such an endeavor would be terrible if attempted. To prevent the cost of enslaving Blacks permanently, he concluded that Africa must be freed through the war. He believed that there was an unusual opportunity to achieve this.

Since Blacks who European white officers trained had helped to save Belgium with the help of their African American brothers and even saved France and conquered German Africa, then the least that Europe could do to return the favor and depart in a significant way from the world's terrible history between 1441 and 1861, was to ensure that a remarkably free central African state was created out of German East Africa and the Belgium Congo. He felt that Belgium ought to be eager to give up the Congo because they suffered from Germany just as much as Africa had.

He further encouraged England to refrain from taking over German East Africa or handing it back. He believed that either could lead to an increased modern effort to restore the efficiency of Africa. This land gave the Iron Age to the world and had been at the forefront in metalworking, agriculture, and weaving for many decades. Du Bois believed that the world at the time had a chance that had not been witnessed since the fifteenth century and that efforts that would engender a new and sincere start in Africa would be outstanding.

The effect of such an effort would be felt by millions of Africans and their descendants around the world. About 30 million individuals from Africa were in the West Indies and South America – these were individuals who had given industry and romance to the West Indies, literature and freedom to Brazil, and art, music, and human sensibility to North America. He stated that among the new nations that would emerge after the war would eventually be a new Africa and a new beginning of culture for the Black race.[46]

As a former president of the American Bar Association, Storey was always available to work on projects to improve different aspects of life, the judiciary, and the legislature. He spoke concerning the legal procedure in the U.S. and pointed out issues facing the legal system at the time. One such issue was that there were too many existing laws, and there was a need to administer the available laws wisely. While admitting that delays in the delivery of justice were required, the prolonged delay was unnecessary and would lead to injustice.

He backed up his points with real-life cases where such issues were identified to ensure that his statements were verified. Storey did not just discuss the judiciary's problems; he also preferred solutions that he believed would help deal with most of the issues. In other speeches he gave, he enlightened his audience on who Emerson was and talked about his honest opinions, which he learned from Emerson's private journals. He was not only influenced by Emerson's strong commitment toward the abolition cause; he educated his audience on his true values regarding several aspects of life.

LEGAL BATTLES AND VICTORIES

First Step to Voter Rights for African Americans (Guinn v. U.S. – 1915)

S TOREY WAS AMONG the prominent Americans who accepted the call of Mary White Ovington to protest the Springfield riots on the 100th anniversary of Lincoln's birth. This was the meeting that eventually led to the establishment of the NAACP. Apart from the *Quinn vs. United States* case, Storey, while serving as the president of NAACP in the early 1910s, successfully ended the exclusion of Blacks from the American Bar Association. Based on his knowledge of history and law, he did not fail to argue against the high level of white racial superiority prevalent at the time.

In his opinion, the primary factor behind the lower status of minorities in the U.S. was mistreatment and the unequal opportunities in the country. Storey disclosed that one primary explanation for southern predisposition to violence and discriminatory legislation was strong evidence that they were bothered about the chances of Black achievement. While serving as the NAACP president, Storey was not involved in the daily functioning of the Association; however, his legal skills undoubtedly proved invaluable.

One of the ideas he strongly promoted was that it was possible to secure civil rights through the courts. While serving as the NAACP legal counsel, Storey fought against the idea that the federal government could not prevent private discrimination and strongly argued that segregation was unconstitutional. This explains why he served as the Association's counsel in its first three crucial cases before the U.S. Supreme Court, including *Guinn v. U.S.* (1915).[47,72,73]

In 1907, the state of Oklahoma was admitted into the Union. Shortly after that, the state passed an amendment to its constitution. The amendment required that citizens were expected to pass a literacy test before being allowed to vote. But there was another clause to the state's Voter Registration Act of 1910, which allowed voters to vote without taking the test as long as their grandfathers had either been qualified to vote before January 1, 1866, were formally residents of "some foreign nation," or had been soldiers. This clause rarely affected white voters but significantly disenfranchised many African American voters, since most of their grandfathers were enslaved before 1866 and therefore ineligible to vote.

Like it was applied in several states, literacy tests were highly subjective. The questions asked were worded confusingly and with several possible correct answers. Another issue with the literacy test was that the tests were graded by white election officials who had already been taught to discriminate against African American voters. An excellent example of the level of discrimination that existed then, as revealed by the U.S. Circuit Court, was the disqualification of an African American graduate even though he was undoubtedly literate and therefore entitled to vote.

Immediately after the November 1910 midterm election, two Oklahoma election officials, Frank Guinn and J.J. Beal, were charged with conspiring to disenfranchise African American voters fraudulently, violating the Fifteenth Amendment. The "grandfather clause" case in which the NAACP filed an amicus brief was the first significant involvement of the Association on the legal battlefront. Storey represented the NAACP in this case. He argued that those who were effectively debarred from voting due to the grandfather clause were African Americans, since many were unable to read. In addition, the clause did not impose the same disability on illiterate whites if their ancestors voted in 1866.[71]

In its ruling, the Supreme Court admitted that a literacy test alone was permissible; however, its joinder with the grandfather clause violated the Fifteenth Amendment's requirement that voting rights should not be denied or abridged based on race, color, or former conditions of servitude.

In its argument, the state of Oklahoma pointed out that its state constitutional amendment made in 1907 was validly passed and was within the state's powers as provided by the Tenth Amendment. The Tenth Amendment reserved all powers not precisely granted to the U.S. government in Article 1, Section 8 of the Constitution to the people or states (Longley, 2020). According to Storey and his NAACP colleagues, the decision of the Supreme Court "was a very great victory . . . a great step in advance [indicating] that the Court has waked up to the situation." [48]

By overturning Oklahoma's grandfather clause while upholding the right of the state to require literacy tests, the Supreme Court eventually confirmed the historical rights of states to enforce voter qualifications provided it did not in any way violate the Constitution of the United States. This ruling was not just a victory for Storey and the NAACP but a symbolic legal victory for African American voting rights. However, the Guinn ruling failed to enfranchise southern Black citizens immediately.

The court ruling further nullified similar voter qualification provisions in the constitutions of other states, like North Carolina, Georgia, Alabama, Virginia, and Louisiana. Although the ruling made it impossible to apply grandfather clauses, the poll taxes and various ways of restricting African American voters were enacted. The *Guinn vs. U.S.* case, which was decided in 1915, was a remarkable legal step in the Civil Rights Movement toward achieving racial equality in the U.S. Storey played a considerable role in securing this success. The remaining legal barriers that denied African Americans the right to vote under the Fifteenth Amendment were eventually outlawed with the passage of the Voting Rights Act of 1965. [49]

The Buchanan v. Warley Case (1917)

Storey's dedication to civil equality was most visible and remarkable in his role in the legal preparations of *Buchanan v. Warley (1917)*, a case of residential segregation. African Americans were prohibited from purchasing houses on blocks with more white residents by a 1914 Louisville, Kentucky city ordinance. At the same time, whites were banned by the same ordinance from purchasing houses on blocks where most of those who lived there were African Americans.

It was common to see black live-in servants with wealthy white homeowners, and the Louisville ordinance allowed this situation. Tension arose not because African Americans lived nearby but because African Americans lived nearby *as equals*. Part of the function of the ordinance was to protect the value of properties owned by whites, which they tended to dump on the market the moment Blacks moved into such neighborhoods. The African American community in Louisville was angered by this ordinance and consequently formed a local chapter of the NAACP. Then they came up with a test case involving a white man who was sympathetic to the cause, Charles H. Buchanan, and William Warley, an African American newspaper editor who was an active member of the local NAACP.[50]

In a bid to challenge the law, Warley accepted to purchase a house owned by Buchanan. According to the provisions of the contract of purchase:

> *"It is understood that I am purchasing the above property for the purpose of having erected thereon a house which I propose to make my residence, and it is a distinct part of this agreement that I shall not be required to accept a deed to the above property or to pay for said property unless I have the right under the laws of the state of Kentucky and the city of Louisville to occupy said property as a residence."*

But Warley failed to pay for the house even after the contract and explained that the law prevented him from buying the property.[51] This made the white seller sue Warley for breach of contract. Of course, the Kentucky Supreme Court upheld the ordinance and made a declaration that Warley should not make payments for the property, so the case was taken to the U.S. Supreme Court.

It is interesting to note that the posture of the case was odd. A white man sued an African American to compel him to buy his property in a neighborhood occupied mainly by whites. The implication was that if Storey succeeded with the case and Buchanan won, the victory would be for all African Americans living in the United States.[51]

The Supreme Court simplified the question as, "May the occupancy, and, necessarily, the purchase and sale of property of which occupancy is an incident, be inhibited by the States, or by one of its municipalities, solely because of the color of the proposed occupant of the premises?"[51]

Storey represented Warley before the Supreme Court, and he contended that the ordinance hindered Blacks of legal rights. According to Storey, the ordinance had negative social consequences for African Americans and not for whites. He argued that:

> "A law which forbids a Negro to rise [does not] forbid a white man to fall," and it is "the common law right of every landowner to occupy his house or to sell or let it to whomever he pleases."
> (Buchanan v. Warley)

Storey suggested that racial purity was simply a myth and residential segregation violated the Fourteenth Amendment's equal protection and "privileges and immunities." He added that it also violated the property rights of African American property owners.[51]

In its ruling, the Court failed to limit the Fourteenth Amendment to the rights of African Americans and other minorities. The Court noted that even when the purpose of the Fourteenth Amendment was to protect African Americans, the broad language was believed to be enough to protect all individuals – white, African American, or other minorities – against discriminatory legislation by the States. Consequently, under the Fourteenth Amendment, Buchanan enjoyed as much right to sell his property as Warley, the African American, did to purchase a property.

However, this case did not result in housing integration. White landowners prevented possible integration via restrictive covenants that the Court also approved based on the same theory that approved Buchanan's right to sell his property. Although people were free to sign restrictive covenants after 1948, the courts could not enforce them, so anyone could also break the covenant without the fear of being taken to court.[51]

Despite several criticisms of the case, it was a favorable turning point in the attitude of the courts toward Blacks. Records show that between 1868 and 1910, a total of twenty-eight cases involved Blacks and the Fourteenth Amendment, and African Americans lost twenty-two. But things changed after the case. Between 1920 and 1943, out of twenty-seven Fourteenth Amendment cases before the Supreme Court, African Americans won twenty-five.[52,53]

Negroes Beg Lives of Supreme Court (1919–1922)

In the late hours of September 1919, sharecroppers assembling at a church in Elaine, Arkansas, were aware of the risk involved in what they were doing. They were unhappy with the unfair low wages they were receiving and sought the assistance of a popular white attorney from Little Rock. The goal was for the attorney to help them get a fairer share of the profits from their efforts. Landowners were fond of requesting obscene shares of the profits every season without providing the sharecroppers proper accounting and even hooked them with supposed debts.

These Black tenant farmers had little chance of redress to this kind of exploitation. On the contrary, as revealed by Megan Ming Francis in *Civil Rights and the Making of the Modern American State,* there was an unwritten law that no African American would be allowed to leave until their debts were settled. The farmers were aware of the dangers involved in their meeting and demands, especially after the racially motivated violence in that location. They armed themselves with rifles.

However, by 11:00pm, white men believed to be affiliated with the local law enforcement fired several shots into the church, and the Black farmers returned the shots. This led to the death of one white man. The issue led to rumors that the sharecroppers had planned an insurrection against whites living in Phillips County. This led to the killing of about 200 Blacks, and the killing was recorded as indiscriminate since men, women, and children were slaughtered in the process.

Five white men also lost their lives, and someone had to be responsible for their deaths. Consequently, twelve Blacks were charged with murder, and no white man was tried for any crime despite the number of deaths.[54]

On January 9, 1923, the Supreme Court received litigation from the Arkansas riots. The National Association for the Advancement of Colored People brought the case on behalf of Frank Moore and eleven other African Americans who were sentenced to death, having been accused of murdering Clinton Lee, the only white man that lost his life during the crossfire.[55] This case is part of the number of occasions when Storey was actively involved in fighting for the rights of Blacks in the United States.

He appeared as counsel for the African Americans while still serving as the president of the NAACP, and Attorney General Utley represented the State in the case. The counsel to the African Americans explained on behalf of the Blacks that they all gathered in their church, located at Hoop Spur, to determine how tenant farmers could relieve themselves of conditions they believed amounted to peonage. However, while they were still gathered, the church where the African Americans assembled was surrounded by armed white men who fired on them. The gunshots, which they claimed were fired by the white men, led to the death of several Black people.

On behalf of the state, it was contended that the Blacks gathered in the church with the sole purpose of planning how to massacre white men. They further claimed that the white men fired shots to deter the Black men from carrying out their plans and to quell a riot. The State contested the jurisdiction of the Supreme Court to consider the appeals based on the fact that:

"Mere errors in point of law, however serious, committed by a criminal court in the exercise of its jurisdiction over a case properly subject to its cognizance, cannot be reviewed by habeas corpus."

During the presentation of the cases, several questions were asked by the justices. Most of the questions were mainly focused on the issue of jurisdiction. The only two expressions from the bench indicated the view of the justices. Justice McReynolds disclosed in substance that the arguments made by Storey on behalf of the African American prisoners who were condemned, in his view, reflected a highly regrettable situation, and it appeared that appropriate steps had not been taken by their counsel to get a review of the cases.

For Justice Holmes, the situation seemed to be one that in the interest of justice, required the Supreme Court to inquire whether it was not warranted in taking jurisdiction without halting at technicalities. One issue that Storey focused on during the case was the alleged "inhumane" treatment that the African Americans received while they were being compelled to make confessions regarding the case.

On the other hand, Godwin, the State's Assistant Attorney General, focused his argument mainly on the legal phases of the case. He strongly contended that counsel for the African Americans, Storey, had failed to pursue the appropriate course in his quest to get a review of the case. He argued that the case needed to be thrown out by the Supreme Court since it was not brought before it in the correct way. He asserted that instead of the counsel of the Blacks to seek an appeal by habeas corpus proceedings, the case was supposed to be brought up on writs of error, adding that this was a tactical mistake that could not be corrected.

The NAACP provided a review of the brief they presented before the Supreme Court. In the review, the Association made charges that were connected to the Arkansas riot of 1919, which involved newspapers, Rotary Club, the courts of the State of Arkansas, the Robert L. Kitchens Post of the American Legion, leading citizens, and other organizations of Helena Ark. In the review, Storey accused them all of attempting to railroad five African Americans to death and using torture to compel the prisoners to falsely testify.

He further alleged that the trial, which was concluded in less than an hour, was mainly dominated by mob hysteria. Storey went on to add that the cause of the cases was an attempt by African American farmers to get legal redress against debt slavery, or peonage, under the crop sharing system that was common in Arkansas. Also, the brief strongly criticized the Supreme Court of Arkansas, stating:

"That for this court to say that they cannot assume that they (the African Americans) necessarily did not have a fair trial shows clearly that the Supreme Court of Arkansas was itself influenced by the same feeling that influenced the leaders of society throughout the region where these tragedies occurred."

The testimony further cited two white men who were members of the Sheriff's posse. They swore that members of the posse murdered the white man for whose murder the Blacks were convicted, and the African Americans had nothing to do with the killing of the white man. According to the brief, they also swore that they flogged the African American prisoners with straps studded with metal, added strangling drugs to their nostrils, and compelled the Blacks to sit on an electric chair in a bid to force them to testify the way the mob wanted.[55]

It is interesting to note that the defendants' lawyers could obtain reversal of the verdicts reached by the Arkansas Supreme Court in six out of the twelve death sentences regarded as the Ware defendants. The six prisoners were sent back to the lower court, where they were to be retried. Although they were convicted of second-degree murder, the sentence was eventually overturned. However, the sentence of the five remaining defendants was upheld by the Arkansas Supreme Court, which declared that the mob atmosphere and the use of coerced testimony did not in any way hinder the African Americans from due process of the law.

After petitioning for a writ of habeas corpus, the writ was issued by Judge John Ellis Martineau of the Pulaski County chancery court. This enabled the African American prisoners to seek habeas corpus relief in Federal court. Eventually, because the trial atmosphere was mob-dominated, and the testimony provided was coerced by torture, the U.S. Supreme Court vacated the six convictions. The court declared that the Blacks were deprived of due process, which the Fourteenth Amendment required. The prisoners were later freed in 1925 in circumstances described as "under cover of darkness," and the NAACP assisted with the safe exit of the men from the state to save them from being lynched.[56]

One of the verdict's implications was the court's drastic departure from its prolonged hands-off approach to cases of injustice that took place in locations such as Elaine. After the *Moore vs. Dempsey* case, there were more legal victories where federal courts intervened in high-profile, due-process cases involving African American defendants, including *Brown vs. Mississippi* (1936), which ruled on confessions obtained under torture, and several others.[54]

The Nixon v. Herndon Case (1927)

Texas was one state that made serious efforts to preserve the white primary. The state's legislature adopted a statute that explicitly prohibited the participation of African Americans in Democratic primary elections.[60] In 1925, Dr. L.A. Nixon challenged the system that permitted only whites to vote in Texas Democratic primaries after being prevented from voting.[61] But the NAACP was there to assist in this case. Storey also played a crucial role, assisting in preparing the brief for *Nixon v. Herndon (1927)*. Nixon filed a suit claiming the statute had violated the Fourteenth and Fifteenth Amendments.

In a unanimous ruling, the court declared on March 7, 1927, that the Texas white primary in the *Nixon v. Herndon case* was unconstitutional.[61] Although the Supreme Court supported this claim, it did not address the issue of whether the primary elections were to be seen as a private affair, which led to the use of the white primary in Newberry. The case was decided based on the Fourteenth Amendment, that the specific statute of Texas in question indeed violated Nixon's equal protection under the law.[60]

However, for Texas to continue with the practice, all they did was change the wording of the state statute. Texas legislatures eventually modified the statute to read that the Democratic Party of Texas had the power to determine its primary voting qualifications. Again, another suit was filed by Nixon in *Nixon v. Condon (1932)*, challenging the deprivation of his right to vote in primaries. In his case, he argued that the statute violated his Fourteenth Amendment rights.[60] Storey died prior to the second case involving Nixon.

In its ruling, the Supreme Court declared that by making the Democratic party its representative, the state legislature of Texas endorsed a discriminatory practice, so Nixon's Fourteenth Amendment rights had been violated. In every society, it is not always easy to drop discriminatory practices. For instance, those in support of the white primary believed that hiding behind the Newberry judgment because the Democratic party is a private organization could prevent Blacks from getting involved simply by passing its resolution apart from the state legislature. Eventually, in the landmark case *Smith v. Allwright* (1944), the all-white primary was formally prohibited, though it still did not stop discrimination against voting rights.[60]

During his career, Storey engaged in several legal battles; some of these cases had a significant effect on the cause of the African Americans. Although he had always fought against racism, lynching, and violence against Blacks, the creation of the NAACP provided a better platform for him to continue his fight for what he believed in. Perhaps one of the earliest achievements was ending the exclusion of African Americans from the American Bar Association. In his view, whites were always coming up with discriminatory legislation and allowing violence to thrive because they were bothered that African Americans could and did achieve success beyond their projection and imagination.

Even though Storey did not participate in the daily activities of the Association, his legal skills were invaluable. They enabled the Association to establish itself as a force equipped to deal with racism, violence, and other challenges facing Blacks at the time. The *Quinn vs. U.S.* case paved the way for African American voting rights, and even though Blacks in the south were not freely allowed to vote after the case, it was indeed a remarkable achievement. His devotion to civil equality was part of why he played a significant role in *Buchanan vs. Warley*. The lawsuit challenged residential segregation, and even though some whites continued to prevent housing integration, this was a significant turning point, especially in how the courts treated African Americans.

It is clear from the four different cases discussed in this chapter that his remarkable legal victories focused on fighting injustice, corruption, and racism. He helped save the lives of the twelve Blacks charged with murder and who were compelled to make confessions later used against them. He played a significant role in ensuring that Blacks were not excluded from participating in Democratic primary elections in *Nixon v. Herndon*. Indeed, his legal skills will always remain part of what helped the NAACP establish itself and fight for the cause of the African Americans.

OTHER REMARKABLE WORKS AND PROPOSALS

The Negro Question (1918)

O n June 27, 1918, Storey delivered an address before the Wisconsin Bar Association entitled *The Negro Question*. It was apparent that one of the primary factors motivating his speech was the mistreatment of African Americans, an issue he was fighting against at the time. Storey understood the judiciary's role in dealing with injustice and racism, which was why he specifically addressed the Wisconsin Bar Association. The address was given while he was the president of the NAACP, which was established nine years before the speech.

He started his address by reminding the audience that every citizen of the United States of America is entitled to enjoy the protection provided by the Fourteenth Amendment against hostile legislation, regardless of race. Despite the provisions made by the U.S. Constitution and laws, African Americans still faced indignities in different forms, and their rights were ignored because of race.

African Americans witnessed brutality on several occasions, like the case of the Springfield riots of 1908 and others. Their rights to vote during elections were violated by factors such as the "grand-father clauses." There was sufficient evidence to prove that the rights of African Americans had been suppressed, and the Southern people further justified this. Blacks were no longer granted the protection of lives and property offered by the law.

They were often at the mercy of a mob when charged with a crime, and, sometimes, they were tortured with impunity and even lost their lives in the process. Unfortunately, even as victims of most of these barbaric acts, Blacks in several states in the U.S. could not get the justice they deserved in courts.

Storey believed that the problem experienced in the U.S. was not the African Americans, "the Negro Problem," as most whites had claimed, but a white man's problem. He believed that the source of all the problems facing the United States, such as racism, lynching, and deprivation of the rights of the Blacks, was the wicked and senseless prejudice against Blacks.

Storey was interested in highlighting the challenges African Americans were facing and the actions of whites against African Americans. Still, he was also interested in how whites in the U.S. could recognize the rights they gave to Blacks. This was why he asked how whites could be induced to enforce the laws they made for protecting Blacks. He was interested in knowing how whites could allow African Americans to enjoy equal opportunity and receive a proper education. Storey advocated that African Americans would be used as a perfect example of civilization instead of making them symbols of medieval brutality.

In his view, the future of the United States depended significantly on their ability to make the average white realize how wicked, cowardly, and cruel their treatment of African Americans, who had lesser resources and were even fewer in number, had been over the years.

He further strengthened his clamor for Blacks to be allowed to vote by talking about the impact of suppressed African American votes on the outcome of elections. According to Storey, African American votes were absolutely suppressed. Although they were counted as eligible voters who would determine the number of representatives every state should have, they were prevented from voting. So, every Democrat had more influence in the outcome of elections than voters in Massachusetts and Wisconsin, since they voted for themselves and one or more African Americans.

Voters in Wisconsin and Massachusetts cast one ballot each; voters cast two or more votes in the Southern states. Storey believed that many individuals in those days used the phrase that "the South is in the middle" in the country's political situation because African Americans were not allowed to vote. The South would not influence if Blacks were given a chance to vote.

He was not focused on how good, or bad, the government was, but on how the suppression of Black votes affected the people of Wisconsin and Massachusetts, cutting down on a large chunk of their voting power. His concern, which he shared, was that suppressing Black votes reduced their ability to influence decisions on issues that affected the entire United States. He further pointed out the dangers of leaving a group of individuals who cast votes to which they were not entitled to influence policies and decisions. Storey strongly believed people must recognize the negative impact of the suppression of African American voters on the entire country and insisted that whites should no longer cast votes meant for African Americans.

Another issue he raised had to do with the education of Blacks. To back up his point, he referred to the open letter by the Southern University Race Commission.

"The solution of all human problems ultimately rests upon rightly directed education."

Storey gave examples of the level of disparity between whites and Blacks in terms of education. One of the examples he gave was the report of an investigation published by the Bureau of Education which disclosed the salaries by race. The report revealed that the average expenditure for a white child was $10.32, while for an African American it was $2.89. Such disparity was even worse in some cases. African American schools looked miserable and lacked adequate lighting, sanitation, and comfort. The structures were crowded, and most of their teachers were not adequately trained before receiving a certificate. A certificate was simply a way to provide a Black teacher for the communities.

The lack of education for the African Americans was an issue Storey believed should concern every American. No nation could possess any more remarkable asset than having adequately educated citizens. African Americans needed to be educated to properly function in various fields and the military. Unfortunately, it was disheartening to note that among the thousands of Blacks who were enlisted in the Army at the time and were prepared to lose their lives to protect the U.S., many of them could not write a simple letter to their families. This, he believed, affected the entire country, not just Blacks.

Storey concluded by reminding his audience of the United States' dangers. As lawyers who were more obligated than others to support the law continuously, he firmly believed that they knew the implication of lawlessness and its risks. In his opinion, when lawyers remained silent amid lynching, deprivation of the rights of African Americans, and several crimes committed against Blacks, they must admit that they were indifferent, cowardly, or gave their approval to such evil acts.

He admonished them to not only speak out but to continue to speak out until every community felt their condemnation and until those who engaged in such acts also acknowledged that the country could no longer tolerate such barbaric acts. Perpetrators of such hideous actions would be discouraged from engaging in them when the constituted authorities enforced the law correctly. In case they feared executing their duty, then the community should be prepared to encourage them or even elect more capable men.[62]

The Words of an Eminent Man on the "Passion for Regulative Legislation" (1919)

Storey was concerned about the tendency of the administration at the time to minimize the rights of the citizens while extending and magnifying the government's autocratic powers. He referred to the speech by Woodrow Wilson given while addressing the Commercial Club of Chicago on March 14, 1908. Before sharing his views, he described Wilson as an eminent and sage man.

According to Wilson, a passion for regulative legislation appeared to have gripped the country. This passion gripped the country suddenly like the impulse of impatience, not like a deliberate mission. In the conduct of the country's business enterprises, several cases of abuse emerged, and the government needed to stop such trends via drastic regulation, as was firmly believed by reformers. But the remedial measures the government adopted appeared to most people to be based on what seemed to be a new conception of the province both of law and government.

Wilson expressed concern that the extensive government control undertaken and being regarded lightly by the citizens did not foster the reign of law. Instead, it was up to the discretion and personal judgment of officials in government to regulate the business of stock companies owned by a good number of private individuals supplying the significant investments of thousands of communities. Wilson did not see any remarkable difference in principle between discretionary governmental regulation and governmental ownership.

He believed that governmental commissions could not be more knowledgeable about business than the individuals who carried out the business. Instead, the governmental regulatory interference with business would complete the embarrassment and confusion everyone was experiencing at the time. In Wilson's opinion, the old processes of the law were the more effective ones, even though they were also the most difficult. Storey's quote concluded that as a nation, it was crucial to be clear on the transactions they desired to end and allow the reign of law instead of the reign of government officials.

Storey reminded his audience that they should consider the writer's words while looking at the problems of the railroad. In his view, the railroads had always been managed by individuals, with some of them even starting from the bottom. These, in his words, were men who devoted most of their lives to understanding the railroad business. On the other hand, Storey described the government appointed to control their activities as individuals who were appointed mainly for political reasons.

These persons offered little experience and skill to the task they were assigned to do. He described the situation as like appointing a law student to cross-examine a witness or a grocer to oversee the operation carried out by an experienced surgeon. Although he opined that the analogies he gave were not perfect, they closely described the situation. Storey referred once again to Wilson's words to bolster his points, saying, "Governmental commissions cannot possibly understand business better than those who conduct it."

Storey firmly believed Wilson did not understand the level of danger government control of railroads and wires would cause; that was because at the time he made the speech, the Adamson bill had not been passed. He wondered what would happen now that the brotherhoods of railroad employees had realized their level of influence. Storey asked what would happen if they threatened to vote against the ruling party unless their wages were increased. He wondered if it would be possible for the ruling party to turn down such a request at the expense of their political ruin.

To him, it was apparent that government control or ownership translated into government having power over votes, which they could get at the expense of the public; the same votes that would eventually decide the outcome of an election. He warned that such a fate awaited the United States, where wage earners would request the same wages the government agreed to pay other workers. Storey concluded that the words of Woodrow Wilson were sufficient and that he was not going to further amplify the argument.[15]

Moorfield Storey's Proposal Before Bar Association: Make Strikes Criminal Offence (1919)

While speaking before the Commissioners' Conference on Uniform State Laws, Storey made a case for a law that would make strikes a criminal offense. He emphasized that the logic that had prevented fights and quarrels between people needed to be applied where a group of persons had resolved to cripple the community service to get something from the people. In his words:

"When you consider that the great public service corporations were founded by the public and are given the right of eminent domain, and all those things which are provided for the accommodation of the public — our water, our food, our heat, our light — is an

amazing thing that the men employed to operate these services should claim that they are the owners of them and have the right to operate them in their own way."

His audience applauded his position on the issue even as he added that it was something impossible that there existed individuals in the body of the community associations that were not ready to regard their contracts as any binding force. He did not fail to express his hopes that the association would make efforts to establish a law that would criminalize strikes. Storey decried the fact that individuals who controlled labor organizations threatened the United States with calamities not even close to the ones that occurred through the acts of Germany.[63]

The League as Safeguard (1919)

Storey was concerned about the different opinions regarding the issue of the Allies of the United States after World War I, as well as the best way to handle the treaty. This was what inspired him to express his views and explained why there was a need to trust allies of the United States to maintain the benefits of the victory.

In Storey's opinion, the increased number of speeches and comments during the time of President Wilson was inspired partly by people's dislike of the methods of the president. He felt that the flow of oratory on both sides was mainly sentimental and expressed fears that people may forget the underlying difficulties of the international situation. He bluntly and briefly reminded his audience that they were not faced with theory but were confronted by a problem. Storey informed his audience that the reason for the war was not to ensure that there was a democracy but to ensure that the world was a safer place for everyone. In his words:

"The German Empire with the war cry 'Weltmacht oder Niedergang,' undertook to make itself ruler of the world. Had it won the war, France would have been dismembered, England stripped of its fleet and its power broken. Holland and Belgium added to Germany, the German colonies restored and enormously enlarged so as to give Germany the control of Africa, and with its

power extending from the North Sea to the Persian Gulf, Germany would have had no world to conquer save the United States."

In his opinion, it was apparent that in the early days of the war, if the Allies had failed to win without assistance, then the U.S. would have been compelled to either join the Allies and fight Germany with their help or fight an already empowered Germany alone (that could have increased her strength from the things taken from her rivals in Europe). He added that at the time, the U.S. was faced with two options – fight the Germans unprepared or pay for several years of inaction by going ahead, under unfavorable circumstances, to create a navy, an army, an air fleet, and other essential items required for modern war.

Storey reminded his audience that even the forts may not have been strong enough to protect the coastal cities against long-range guns. So, he concluded, the reason the U.S. went to war was simply that staying neutral would have led to destruction. While it was crucial to conquer Germany to save the U.S., he explained that it was also essential to ensure that Germany remained weak and was prevented from developing a powerful combination of nations to guarantee the victory already achieved. In his opinion, Germany was capable of dominating Russia and the Balkan States (perhaps with the assistance of Japan, a country the U.S. had tried to isolate) within a decade if adequate measures were not taken immediately.

He observed that France could not have been able to resist such a combination by Germany despite the support of England since their population was half that of Germany. The solution was to set up barriers that would help curtail the ambitions of the Germans. He remarked that the resolution adopted, the creation of a combination of civilized nations with sufficient power to prevent Germany from renewing efforts that had been foiled with their united strength, was an excellent one.

This resulted in the creation of Czechoslovakia, Poland, and Yugoslavia. Still, he also added that the newly created states could not stand unless they received the support of great nations for some years. The support given to these states was not just for their sake but also for the U.S. Storey believed these newly created nations served as fortification for the U.S. against German aggression, both on the Southern and Eastern fronts. So, he advocated that the treaty that created the new countries should also support them.

To establish a permanent barrier against German ambition and desire for revenge, he suggested that it was crucial to establish the League of Nations. Without such power behind the treaty, the treaty was merely a "scrap of paper." He felt that the U.S. seemed to overlook the fact that the provisions establishing the League of Nations were crucial to protecting the U.S. Storey believed there was a need to develop the League on the confidence in honesty and loyalty of every member if it was going to succeed. According to Storey:

> *"If the attempt to defeat the treaty succeeds, we shall be left without allies and face to face with the necessity of preparing for our own defense – a preparation involving an expense which is appalling and consequences to our people which are equally to be dreaded."*

In Storey's opinion, the treaty was equally essential for the protection of the U.S. as it was for victory in the war. Suppose there was a need for an amendment. In that case, it should be carried out easily via a conference with allies, instead of through new negotiations with governments that had already been embittered by the speeches made by members of the Senate and people's actions. In his final words, Storey stated that what most nations of the world demanded at the time was peace. What the people needed was peace and protection against future war. He emphasized that not even imaginary dangers conjured up to defeat the treaty or a desire for partisan success would be accepted as an excuse for sacrificing the nations' interest by not accepting to ratify the treaty.[64]

Support for Anti-Lynching Bill (1922)

During the thirteenth annual convention of the NAACP, Storey addressed members of the Association and made a case for the passage of the Anti-Lynching bill. He commenced his speech with a question:

> *"With men everywhere striking for higher pay or less work, would*

a strike for life and liberty by the negros in the South be wholly unjustifiable?"

He advocated for the passage of the Dyer Anti-Lynching bill before the U.S. Senate. According to Storey, the main reason lynching persisted was that it was still a safe practice. To buttress his point that lynching had flourished because it was safe to practice it, he referred to the words of Henry Watterson:

"It flourishes as an opportunity to indulge in spectacular murder when there is no fear that the next Grand Jury will return murder indictments."

He asserted that lynching would disappear when the American citizens firmly resolved to stop it. He informed his audience that serious conflict may be ahead of them and may eventually be provoked by racial prejudice. He added that the African Americans had managed to be uniformly loyal in every crisis recorded so far.[65]

Moorfield Storey Appears Before Supreme Court for Kansas in Howat Suit (1922)

Oral arguments brought against the State of Kansas relating to two cases that Alexander Howat initiated along with other labor leaders ended on February 28, 1922, in the Supreme Court. The purpose of these cases was to determine the validity of the statute that established the Court of Industrial Relations. As the counsel for Kansas, Storey asserted that the State was entitled to the same right to protect itself against cases of strikes as it had against possible invasion by a hostile army.

While stating that the citizens should have recourse to the courts to intervene and resolve their disputes, Storey added that labor unions do not have rights, either by strikes or other means, more significant than those enjoyed by other citizens. According to him, although a man's right to walk away from his job could not be denied, "strikes permit people to force a whole community into turmoil." Storey believed that the suppression of strikes would not be "chattel slavery" and could not lead to voluntary servitude. He declared that the law should be the same for labor unions, just as it is for every citizen.

Redmond C. Brennon, counsel for Howat, contended while closing the case that there was a need for a limit upon the exercise of police power. Brennon went on to criticize the law and described it as imposing upon miners' terms from which farmers and other producers had already been exempted. He also denied that coal mining was affected by public use.[66]

Based on the majority of his speeches, Storey was firmly convinced that regardless of the complaints against African Americans at the time, the source of the problem the U.S. was facing – deprivation of the rights of African Americans, lynching, and racism – was due to the unreasonable prejudice against African Americans. Contrary to the opinion of some whites that Blacks were the problem, he believed that it was a white man's problem.

The suppression of African American voters and the deprivation of Blacks from gaining access to quality education had serious, adverse effects on the country. His view was that providing proper education for African Americans and allowing them to vote would help resolve many challenges. Another issue of great concern to Storey was that of strikes by labor unions, where his solution was for the government to make strikes a criminal offense.

THE NAACP

Walter Francis White and the NAACP

ORN ON JULY 1, 1893, Walter Francis White led the National Association for the Advancement of Colored People (NAACP) between 1929 and 1955. He worked with Storey in moving the organization forward, as seen in a sample letter written by Storey about the possibility of the NAACP taking a voting rights case in Texas on January 10, 1925.[56,57]

As an American civil rights activist, he joined the organization as a staff member in 1918 at the invitation of James Weldon Johnson, acting as an investigator. He started his career as the secretary assistant to the NAACP at the organization's national headquarters. This was while Storey was still the president of the association. Although he was only twenty-five years old, W.E.B. Du Bois and other NAACP leaders got over their concerns regarding his age.

White eventually became an undercover agent and was intensely involved in investigating cases of lynching that took place in the South, which were at their peak at the time. He leveraged his appearance to increase the effectiveness of his investigations of cases of lynching and race riots. He always identified with African Americans as one of them and could also "pass" and talk to whites as one of them. His work was undoubtedly hazardous, but he managed to achieve a remarkable level of success. He successfully investigated forty-one cases of lynching, two cases of widespread peonage, and eight race riots.

How did White manage to carry out numerous investigations in his time? It was mainly because of his appearance. He was of mixed race, with European and African ancestry on both sides. However, his dominant features reflected his European ancestry, as he mentioned in his autobiography, *A Man Called White*. According to White:

> *"I am a Negro. My skin is white, my eyes are blue, my hair is blond. The traits of my race are nowhere visible upon me."*

Five out of thirty-two of his great-great-great-grandparents were black, while the rest were whites. Based on the oral history of White's mother, his mother's maternal grandparents were an enslaved woman known as Dilsa and her master, William Henry Harrison. White's great-grandmother Dilsa was Harrison's concubine, and they had six children together. The name of one of their daughters was Marie Harrison, the mother of Madeline White's mother. Harrison was eventually elected as president of the United States.

Marie Harrison, White's grandmother, was Augustus Ware's concubine; she had four children for the wealthy white man who purchased a home for her and transferred some of his wealth to his children. Interestingly, White and his family identified as African Americans and resided among the African American community in Atlanta. While raising their children, White's parents adopted a firm and kind approach to child-rearing. They encouraged hard work and regular schedules. As White mentioned in his autobiography, they had a strict schedule every Sunday, including being locked in his room by his parents for silent prayer.

He described the experience as boring and would plead to do his homework instead. One of the interesting stories of his early days was when he threw a rock at a white kid who had used a derogatory name towards him simply because he drank water from a fountain set aside for African Americans. These are some of the events that helped shape White's self-identity as he started cultivating skills to pass for white, which also assisted him in preserving his safety as a civil rights activist in the South.

The NAACP provided legal defense for the convicted African Americans for the Elaine massacre with Storey as part of the legal team. The ruling of the Supreme Court overturned the initial convictions.

It also established a crucial precedent regarding how trials were conducted. The Supreme Court discovered that the conditions under which the original trial was conducted significantly affected the defendants' rights. Some individuals in the courtroom were armed with a mob waiting outside the court. This was a clear sign of intimidation of the court and the jury.

White gave a more explicit description of the kind of trial that occurred in the details of his publication in the Nation on December 6, 1919. According to White:

> "A Committee of Seven" composed of white citizens of Helena held hearings for the purpose of determining the facts in the case. At least two members of that committee are plantation owners themselves. According to two sources of information, when suspects were brought before this committee, they were seated in a chair charged with electricity. If the Negroes did not talk as freely as the Committee wished, the current was turned on until they did so. This committee has declared that it secured many confessions from Negro suspects, but so far as could be learned none of the details of these confessions has been published." [58]

He carried out these investigations while repeatedly risking his life in the backwaters of Florida, the cotton fields of Arkansas, and the piney woods of Georgia. Over time, White transformed into a master of incognito investigating. Although he did not eventually join the Ku Klux Klan undercover, despite the pressures to do so, he leveraged his access to Klan leaders to enhance his investigation into the activities of the Klan, including the "sinister and illegal conspiracy against human and civil rights."

After the failed attempt by the leader of the Klan, Edward Young Clark, to make him join the Klan, White received signed letters from Clark, which aided his investigations. Clark made more inquiries regarding White's life and stopped sending him letters after learning more of his history. White also received threats from anonymous letters informing him that his life would be in danger if he disclosed the information he had obtained from Clark. White had already submitted the information to the U.S. Department of Justice and the New York Police Department. White believed that his cause would benefit significantly by undermining the hold of mob violence.[59]

In a bid to be popular as a leader, White competed with Marcus Garvey's appeal and learned to showcase a skillful verbal dexterity. In the words of his NAACP successor Roy Wilkins, "White was one of the best talkers I've ever heard." Throughout his career, White consistently spoke against discrimination, segregation, and black nationalism. He was among the founders of the "New Negro" culture, courtesy of his cultural interests and association with white literary power brokers Alfred A. Knopf and Carl Van Vechten. It was popularly regarded as the Harlem Renaissance and was the center of African American intellectual and artistic life.

He was also greatly involved in the plans and organizational structure of the fight against public segregation. He provided President Truman a draft for the executive order used in desegregating the armed forces after the Second World War. Under White's leadership of the NAACP, the organization established its Legal Defense Fund, which successfully challenged cases of segregation and disfranchisement. This campaign was quite successful. One of such cases was the Supreme Court ruling in *Brown v. Board of Education* (1954), which determined that segregated education was unequal.

During his tenure as president of the NAACP, White increased the organization's membership to about 500,000. He was inadvertently deputized during the Tulsa race massacre. He was even told by one of his deputies that he could shoot an African American and the law would be behind him.

To enable him to interview Governor Charles Hillman Brough of Arkansas, who he would not have met as a representative of the NAACP, White had to obtain press credentials from the *Chicago Daily News*. After the interview, White received a letter of recommendation and an autographed photograph from Brough to enable him to meet people. Several threats of lynching an African American "passing for white" forced him to escape on a train after being harbored by some prominent African American families. According to the train conductor, White was leaving "just when the fun is going to start," since they had discovered that there was a "damned yellow nigger down here passing for white, and the boys are going to get him."

When White inquired from the conductor what they would do to the "yellow nigger" if he were caught, the conductor replied, "When they get through with him, he won't pass for white no more!" The phrase "High yellow" referred to African Americans of mixed racial descent and a combination of European features. After his investigations, White published his observations regarding the riot and the trial in the *Chicago Defender*, the *Daily News*, *The Crisis*, the NAACP magazine, and *The Nation*. The Arkansas governor requested that the United States Postal Service prohibit the mailings of *The Crisis* and *Chicago Defender* to Arkansas, and others at the local level also attempted to get an injunction against the spread of the *Defender*.

Although the NAACP published details of crimes committed by whites against Blacks, none were prosecuted, either by local or state southern governments. As president of the NAACP, White strongly supported federal anti-lynching bills and lobbied for them. However, they could not surmount the opposition of the southern Democrats in the Senate. The House passed the Dyer Anti-Lynching Bill in 1922, and this was the first legislation the House of Representatives passed since Reconstruction that specifically shielded African Americans from lynching. Since the Senate was under the control of Southerners who opposed such a bill, Congress failed to pass the Dyer bill.

According to the results of numerous surveys conducted by White, forty-six of fifty cases of lynching within the first six months of 1919 were African American victims, and ten of these victims were burned at the stake. He concluded after the Chicago Race riot of 1919 that the reason for these cases of violence was "prejudice and economic competition" and not the rape of white women by African American men, as was often rumored.

This was also the conclusion of the Chicago city commission after investigating the 1919 riot. Newspapers reported a decline in the number of southern lynchings in the late 1910s; however, there was an increase in postwar violence in northern and midwestern cities due to the competition for housing and work by returning veterans, black migrants, and immigrants. One of the cases of violence White investigated took place in 1918 in Lowndes and Brooks counties, Georgia. It was also one of the worst cases he had investigated. A pregnant African American was tied to a tree and burned alive. The mob did not stop there. They proceeded to split the woman open, and her still-alive baby was thrown to the ground and stomped to death.

During his activities and career, White became an influential figure. This was confirmed by the remarks of senator James F. Byrnes, a segregationist during the Dyer bill. In the words of Byrnes:

"One Negro has ordered this bill to pass. If Walter White should consent to have this bill laid aside its advocates would desert it as quickly as football players unscramble when the whistle of the referee is heard."

The only thing that kept the bill before Congress at the time was White's word, and even though the bill failed to pass the Senate, the NAACP, under the leadership of White, managed to record widespread public support for the cause. According to a 1938 poll by Gallup, seventy-two percent of Americans and fifty-seven percent of Southerners supported an anti-lynching bill. Part of White's achievement included his contribution to establishing alliances among civil rights activists. On March 21, 1955, White suffered a heart attack, and this led to his death at the age of 61 years.[59]

Seventeenth Annual Convention of NAACP (1926)

The NAACP held its Seventeenth Annual Convention in Chicago, and it was a gathering of individuals who desired a future where every African American could enjoy new and fuller freedom. The Association represented authority and tradition, which is why many African Americans – looking forward to the future and fresher and fuller freedom – attended. Held in the Pilgrim Baptist Church, the conference was indeed an important one both from the political and literary point of view. At the time, African Americans could speak with new confidence as they counted the number of public and material achievements made so far. Also, the level of self-consciousness of the African Americans at the time had increased, courtesy of the Great War.

They now knew that amid the most tragic experiences of any given human group, they could sustain the role of a hero. From racial obscurity and being seen by whites as people who may be interesting but not important, the artists in the African Americans emerged; they began to occupy a position of importance. African Americans enjoyed a new level of confidence in American art, with many achievements to celebrate, including the poetry of Langston Hughes and Countee Cullen and the fictional work and musical compositions of Jean Toomer and Walter White.

Although some individuals still saw the African Americans as hewers of wood and drawers of water for a few generations to come, they would still be humanized courtesy of some of their achievements. Just like every other individual, the African American is what he does. The speaker at the conference charged his fellow Blacks to continue with the efforts recorded at the time. Poets should continue to create quality works like that of Mr. Hughes and Cullen. He further charged the African American businessmen to construct cities.

He believed that all white men of goodwill should be happy with the level of progress made so far by Blacks at the time and over the fact that such achievements by African Americans were without white tutelage. He believed that no individual of goodwill would desire to dwell in a society where his inferiors lived, since they would only impoverish them. The speaker concluded by adding that Kant's ideal of human society remains the only ideal:

"A kingdom of autonomous persons, no one of whom may be used as a means for the ends of others, but each one of whom is sovereign, an end in himself, worthwhile for his own sake."

The only way to establish such a kingdom was through rational self-assertion because it can never be delivered as a gift from one group to another.[67]

Southern College President Sees Era of Improved Race Relations (1926)

While delivering an address before those who attended the NAACP conference, Dr. John Hope forecasted an era of new and improved relations between African Americans and whites. He believed that this was because an increasing number of educated whites, most of whom were in colleges and universities at the time, were making efforts to improve race relations. The speaker declared that there were about four groups of persons in the South. The first one consisted of individuals who were outrightly against the African Americans. According to Hope, those who belonged to this group believed that Blacks were unworthy of opportunity or effort.

Those who belonged to the second group desired to give African Americans a better chance mainly for their selfish reasons. Individuals who genuinely and unselfishly wanted to offer colored people better opportunities while adhering to established distinctions belonged to the third class. The last group of persons also happened to be the smallest, but a growing and inspiring one. Those who belonged to this group were primarily young and educated people who were firmly convinced it was possible to offer the African Americans a fair deal based on the American ideal of the square deal. Such could occur without jeopardizing the country's interest or that of any other group in the country.

Hope believed that those belonging to the fourth group represented the most significant and inspiring movement in race issues in the South at the time. He was hopeful and expectant that the section of the country where he lived would become less provincial. The average African American would be allowed to come in and enjoy their fair share of democratic, fundamental, and better consideration based on the improved spirit of liberality.

Hope believed that the second and most encouraging sign of the new era of race relations, which he forecasted, was a group of individuals he referred to as generous and unselfish. He believed those who belonged to this small group would eventually exert the same level of substantial influence as other righteous minorities. Among the people who belonged to this small group were the most liberal individuals and young, educated women and men.

Hope concluded his speech by stating that things were already improving because, at the time, African Americans were gradually receiving better protection in courts and from police officers. The school facilities being provided had increased. The number of instances where two races in the South enjoyed better opportunities to gather for conferences and freely talk and take actions together to achieve a common goal also increased.[68]

NAACP Information (1929)

Publicity and Publications

Here are quick facts regarding the activities of the NAACP during the early years of operation. In 1919, the total number of *"The Crisis,"* published every month by the NAACP, was 98,908 copies. Also, the total number of works of literature (including *The Crisis*) distributed by the NAACP in 1920 was about 1,002,988. To find out more about the publicity and publications of the NAACP, check the standard statistical work on the subject, entitled, *Thirty Years of Lynching.* The total number of miles officers of the NAACP traveled in 1919 was 101,069, the equivalent of crossing the earth's circumference four times.

In 1921, the organization held over 2,000 big meetings and several smaller ones. Also, NAACP officers addressed 656 public meetings (about two public meetings daily). NAACP's press publicity also reached the most crucial white newspapers and major news distributing agencies in the U.S. during this period.

The NAACP news releases were published in virtually all parts of the world, including Japan and European countries. About 250 colored newspapers in the U.S. received a regular weekly press service on issues affecting race relations. *The Shame of America* advertisement, which was in half and full-page displays, was placed in western, northern, and southern newspapers with the widest circulations. It reached over 5 million individuals, both in the U.S. and abroad, who had been unaware of the crucial facts and figures regarding lynching. This is perhaps the most significant single strike of publicity propaganda ever made in the quest for justice for African Americans.

Eternal Vigilance

The records regarding the significant accomplishments of the NAACP can only be partial since it would be difficult to provide a complete account. Even in the absence of these achievements and without the constant efforts being made to secure broader opportunity and complete fulfillment made by the U.S. to all races, the organization can still justify itself with its ability to watch over the rights which African Americans now enjoy. The truth is that people of color need someone that will always be on guard, and that person is an organization – the NAACP. "Eternal Vigilance Is the Price of Liberty."

Common justice and equality of opportunity for African Americans are crucial for white Americans and people of color.

The NAACP operates based on the reasonable assumption that the documents are adopted literally and precisely at their face value. The organization welcomes the cooperation of all Americans regardless of race in ensuring that they are directly and strictly true in their application to present-day America. On its twelve-year record, the NAACP sought the support and cooperation of everyone to ensure that the democracy being preached was practiced as thoroughly as possible. It is a responsibility that no single American can avoid because it has to do with the life of democracy and the entire nation.

Membership fees and contributions are the primary sources of funds for the NAACP, and there is no limit to the amount anyone can contribute. Here is a breakdown of the membership fees for the organization:

- Annual: $1
- Blue certificate: $5
- Gold certificate: $10
- Contributing $25 or more

Contact the organization for more information if you are interested in becoming a member. Also, you can write the national office to get more information and permission to establish a branch if none exists in your community. If you know that you cannot work, you can also support the NAACP by making your contributions available to the Association.

Key Officers of the NAACP in its Early Days

Here is a list of the national officers who piloted the Association's affairs.

National Officers:

- **President:** Moorfield Storey
- **Vice Presidents:** Rev. John Haynes Holmes, Archibald H. Grimke, Bishop John Hurst, Arthur B. Spingarn, Oswald Garrison Villard, and Mary B. Talbert.

Executive Officers:

- **Chairman of the Board:** Mary White Ovington
- **Treasurer:** J. E Spingarn
- **Editor of the Crisis:** Dr. W.E.B. Du Bois
- **Director of Branches:** Robert W. Bagnall
- **Field Secretaries:** William Pickens and Addie W. Hunton
- **Secretary:** James Weldon Johnson
- **Assistant Secretary:** Walter White

The History, Achievements, and Purposes of the NAACP, and Why You Should Join

Why was the NAACP established? It was undoubtedly founded in response to the issues facing people of color in the United States. About 4,000 people have been lynched in the U.S. in thirty-four years, including eighty-three women. In 1922, sixty-four cases of lynching took place, and people were roasted alive publicly. The NAACP was also established to champion issues and challenges, such as segregation laws, the Ku Klux Klan, "Jim Crow" on the railways, peonage, and disenfranchisement.

The Object – Justice

The primary reason the Association exists is to combat the persecution that African Americans have suffered in the United States and to preserve their civil and legal rights and their full potential. The Association is also focused on helping to secure for people of color equality of opportunities with other citizens. In summary, NAACP was established to make 12,000,000 Americans:

- Physically liberated from peonage
- Mentally free from ignorance
- Politically liberated from disfranchisement
- Socially free from insult

How it Began

The Association started as a small committee in 1909 with Lincoln's birthday call, which was written by Oswald Garrison Villard and signed by fifty-four individuals, including Charles Edward Russell, Mary White Ovington, John E. Milholland, Rabbi Stephen S. Wise, Dr. John Haynes Holmes, Francis J. Grimke, and several others.

What did the Association achieve in 12 years?

Within twelve years of its existence, by 1923, the Association had established 434 branches in forty-four states and the Dominion of Canada. Also, its membership grew to 110,000, with a gross expenditure of $72,511.72 for the year 1922. Here is a summary of some of the significant achievements of the NAACP:

- **Residential Segregation:** A unanimous decision of the U.S. Supreme Court, on November 5, 1917, declared the ordinance passed in Louisville, Kentucky, unconstitutional. Moorfield Storey, president of the NAACP, handled the case on behalf of the Association.

- **The Grandfather Clauses:** In 1915, when the "Grandfather Clause" in state constitutions that disfranchised African Americans was brought before the U.S. Supreme court, it was declared unconstitutional. Moorfield Storey submitted the only brief filed by a private organization or individual, and it was filed for the NAACP.

- **Fight Against Peonage:** On January 9, 1923, Storey argued the cases of five African Americans in the U.S. Supreme Court. They were sentenced to death in connection with the 1919 Arkansas riots. In a decision rendered on February 19, the convictions were reversed. Also, the fate of another six men who were sentenced to death hinged on these cases, and a total of $14,000 was spent by the Association on these cases.

- **Disfranchisement of Blacks:** Officers representing the Association at hearings before the Census Committee of the House of Representatives pointed out flagrant disfranchisement of colored people in the South.

- **Extradition of Blacks:** The extradition of colored men to southern states accused of various crimes where there was a higher chance of them being lynched was successfully prevented by the Association in several cases. This eventually attracted national and international attention to the failure of common justice for African Americans in the lynching states.

- **Tulsa Riot:** Within six hours after the news regarding the Tulsa riot reached New York, Assistant Secretary Walter White investigated the situation and published his findings throughout the country. Consequently, the Association raised and expended about $3,646.54 as fund relief.

Ku Klux Klan

The Association also commenced a publicity campaign against the Ku Klux Klan, which the New York World took up. The NAACP revealed its facts to the world and did not stop its campaign. This was instrumental to the barring of *The Birth of a Nation,* a movie that glorified the Klan and was also used as Klan propaganda, in California, Boston, and other places. The NAACP adequately represented these cities. In December 1922, representatives of the Association appeared before the New York State Censorship Commission, which led to the cutting out of objectionable aspects of the film.

Lynching

The NAACP was the first organization to start an intensive, systematic, and organized fight against lynching in the U.S. During the campaign in 1916, the Association raised $10,000 as an anti-lynching fund. Over $40,000 was spent by the Association between 1916 and 1923 in the fight against lynching. Several NAACP investigators risked their lives to visit scenes of lynching where they acquired facts and, in some cases, managed to establish the innocence of the victim and published the facts to the world. The Association's anti-lynching campaign culminated in the Dyer Anti-Lynching Bill on January 26, 1922, by the House of Representatives.

It also resulted in a favorable report of the Bill by the Committee on the Judiciary of the Senate, but it was abandoned due to filibuster by southern senators. While fighting for the Dyer Bill, the Senate received a memorial organized and presented by the Association. The memorial was signed by thirty-nine city mayors, twenty-four state governors, two former U.S. attorney generals, eighty-eight bishops in addition to key churchmen, nineteen state Supreme Court Justices, and several others. According to former Senator Burton of Ohio, the petition was the most impressive document presented to the Senate. Part of the effect of the persistent efforts made by the Association against lynching was that it aroused public sentiment and made it a national issue. It also emphasized the importance of taking steps toward abolishing lynching by the southern states.

Legislation

The Association opposed several discriminatory laws, such as segregation and anti-intermarriage laws. In January 1923, the NAACP received assurances from Senator Capper that the anti-intermarriage provision of the Federal Marriage and Divorce Bill, which he initially introduced, would be stricken out. Also, at the instance of the Association, several civil rights bills were introduced in some states, and one of them was enacted into law in Michigan.

Miscellaneous

During the war, the NAACP pushed for the training and commissioning of African American officers instead of discrimination against Black soldiers. President Harding received a petition signed by 50,000 persons on behalf of African American soldiers of the 24th Infantry who were summarily condemned after the Houston riot. Ever since the petition was submitted, the War Department investigated each case, and some of the convicted men were released. Also, on January 31, 1923, there were announcements of several instances of commutation of life sentences. Segregation was also opposed in schools, railways, theatres, restaurants, motion picture theatres, and other public places.[69]

The Death of Moorfield Storey (1929)

On October 24, 1929, *The New York Times* announced the passing of Moorfield Storey, a former president of the American Bar Association. According to the details of the publication, Storey died in the night at his residence in Lincoln. He was dealing with an illness that had lasted several months until his death at the age of 85. *The New York Times* observed that Storey's death was a distinct shock to many of his friends, since most of them were not aware he was dealing with a serious illness. Storey had two sons, Richard C. Storey and Charles M. Storey. He also had two daughters, Mrs. R. W. Lovett and Mrs. E. J. Burke.

About two years after Storey's death, his son, a Boston Attorney, died. Richard Cutts Storey, who died on June 10, 1931, at his summer camp in Farmington, Maine, had dealt with a health issue for some time. He was fifty-seven years old and a member of the Boston law firm of Storey, Thorndike, Palmer & Dodge. He had four sons and a daughter, and his wife's name was Miss Anna Ladd.

Storey's funeral service was held at Kings Chapel. Those present to pay their last tribute to Storey included representatives of the nation, state, and city. *The New York Times* described Storey as a popular man for his views regarding various issues of national importance, as well as his interest in affairs of the state and city. According to *The New York Times*, he was "a champion of the rights of negros." His law practice began in Boston after serving as private secretary to Charles Sumner.

He was also one of the leaders of the American Bar for close to two generations. He became the president of the NAACP in 1910 and, as described by F. Lauriston Bullard in an article published in *The New York Times* in 1927, Storey was "known in many lands for his defense of the weak and oppressed." His consistent and repeated insistence that the U.S. grant the Philippines independence while serving as an honorary president of the Indian Rights Association reflects his tendency to support the cause of the minority side.

This tendency is also shown in his presidency of the Anti-Imperialistic League in the last 24 years and fighting the cause of the African Americans in crucial litigation. Perhaps the most significant evidence of his tendency to fight the cause of the weaker side is the Corrigan-Curtis case before the Supreme Court of the U.S. in January 1926. Storey was also a president of the Massachusetts Reform Club, former editor of the *American Law Review*, vice president of the National Civil Service Reform League, and president of the Massachusetts Bar Association.

Storey was also the overseer of Harvard College in 1877, 1888, and from 1892 to 1910. Storey served as counsel for the State of Kansas, the New Haven Railroad, the Chemical Foundation Inc., and several other prominent clients during his career. He was the author of *Life of Charles Sumner.* In the American series, he wrote *The Reform of Legal Procedure* and *Problems of Today,* which embodied, respectively, the Godkin lectures he delivered at Harvard College and the Storrs lectures he gave at the Yale Law School. Storey was also the author of *The Negro Question* and *The Conquest of the Philippines.*[70]

The NAACP recorded great successes after it was formed in 1908, and the documented successes were made possible by the efforts and sacrifices of several individuals. Walter Francis White was among those who risked their lives to fight the cause of the African Americans. His appearance enabled him to investigate several cases of lynching and race riots since he could conveniently be regarded as white. Despite the dangers involved with the kind of work he did at the time, he did not relent in his efforts to unravel the injustice and inhumane acts of violence against African Americans.

Apart from Storey's efforts to stop the issue of lynching, he was also involved in the fight against public segregation. His zeal and dedication to the cause of the NAACP yielded great results as membership of the Association increased during his tenure as president of the NAACP. The Association was undoubtedly left in good hands even as Storey passed away in 1929. He would always be remembered by the African Americans, the Filipinos, and all those who believed in equal rights and fairness to others. Indeed, he lived an impactful life and left a legacy that has continued to inspire men and women in different locations worldwide.

CONCLUSION

IT WOULD BE impossible to talk about all the achievements, challenges, and victories of Moorfield Storey in one book; however, we can say that he lived a successful life. As a lawyer, Storey excelled, but not by the knowledge of the books. He was in the front rank as an advocate, and he possessed a rare common sense as an adviser. From the professional point of view, we can see him as an excellent example of an individual that should be emulated. Although a few men were able to record such achievements in his time, while examining the life of Storey, we think beyond his accomplishments.

He was a remarkable citizen at the community level because he truly molded public opinion. In his time, it was generally believed that a person served his country best in public life. Public office requires specific qualities that many individuals with extraordinary abilities lack, while others are not ready to acquire such traits. It is good to know that even though men with such qualities are few, every democratic community is always blessed with citizens who turn out to be molders of public opinion, even without holding office. A democracy cannot survive without such individuals.

These are courageous people; they think clearly and have the public spirit. Such men demand nothing for themselves – emolument or honor – and are only concerned about the public good. Their voice constantly proclaims their opinions fearlessly, and these are indeed the great hope of democracy. Moorfield Storey was one such man.

Although he once ran for Congress unsuccessfully, he never held an elective public office and was never a candidate for one. However, in all issues – of men or politics – Storey played a valiant part not as a public office holder but as a private citizen. He did not restrain himself from antagonizing those he regarded as local demagogues.

He played his part in every cause that came on to the political scene, including wholeheartedly supporting Cleveland during the Blaine campaign. He was vice president of the National Civil Service League and the Massachusetts Civil Service Association president. The predominant trait of his character – an intense empathy for the downtrodden or underdog – was greatly intensified while he was serving under Charles Sumner. Throughout his days on earth, Storey was a friend of the African Americans. He was vocal in denouncing lynching and other atrocities caused by painful and unfortunate racial hatred.

When he assumed the post of President of the newly formed National Association for the Advancement of Colored People (NAACP) in 1910, he fought for the rights of African Americans before the United States Supreme Court. As amicus curiae, Storey argued in the *Guinn vs. US* case and the "grandfather clause" was eventually declared uncon-stitutional. In 1916, he successfully prevented segregation in Louisville and his last appearance was also in defense of African Americans where it was declared that a group of Blacks were not convicted by the due process of law.

The most remarkable tribute to the nobility with which Storey endeavored to translate his sympathy for the underdog into action was the silent presence at his memorial service of individuals he had spent his entire life defending. Although we can state clearly that the best example of his devotion to the oppressed was the cause of the African Americans, he was in the same manner zealous for the Indians and Armenians. It was therefore not a surprise when he also lent his voice and wrote in support of the independence of the Philippines. It did not matter whether he believed or not in all the causes he fought for. There must always be differences of opinion, and there is still no end to such cases as the issue of racism.

The tribute we pay to Storey is to the courage with which he stayed focused on his opinions, his intense sympathy with humanity, and to the fact that he could forget himself and his fortune in his quest to defend the oppressed in society. These qualities made Storey unique, especially in these modern times when it is often easier to go with popular opinion.

Of course, just like every other human being, he also had his limitations, and there were defects in his qualities. For instance, he was impatient with opposition and was perhaps not always tolerant in the heat of controversy in some cases. Maybe he also failed to appreciate the good faith of his adversaries, but his feelings were only natural to an individual of his disposition. When he was unduly critical of the conduct of public men or his opponents, it was mainly because he was unafraid, bold, and a fighter who adopted a cautious and concili-atory approach. Without thought of personal popularity, Storey met his opposition head-on in court and was not the type that modified the expression of his views in a bid to find favor with his auditors.

Indeed, some of these limitations were temporary and only brought the strength of his character to the limelight. Storey possessed a kindliness in hospitality, a strong capacity for friendship, and always lent a helping hand to people who needed it. His colleagues remem-bered him not just as a successful individual – as the world defines success – but as a person who deployed his talents to the cause of his fellow men. He was described as one "who comprehends his trust, and to the same keeps faithful with a singleness of aim."

Storey lived among others as a great citizen, and he left behind an example that others should follow many years after he was gone. No one doubted the ardor of his partisanship. He was a true crusader, a successful lawyer, and one who engaged in the common, everyday, and inconspicuous things of life that created happiness and brought light to others who, in one way or another, depended on him. What was remarkable about him was not really in the number of friends he had from different locations and of all ages, but perhaps the quality of his friendship. Those who paid tribute to him described his sense of humor as delicious, and he had a rare quality of youthfulness.

Indeed, the most suitable words to estimate the life and character of Moorfield Storey while he lived were also his own words while paying tribute to Charles Sumner in the last chapter of his biography:

"He was a strong force constantly working for righteousness. He had absolute faith in the principles of free government as laid down in the Declaration of Independence, and he gave his life to secure their practical recognition. They were not to him glittering generalities, but ultimate practical truths."

Perhaps, if Storey was afforded the chance to choose his epitaph, he might have repeated the exact words that the poet put in Ben Adhem's mouth – ***"Write me as one who loved his fellow men."***[2]

FINAL THOUGHTS

O NE OF THE most remarkable addresses made by Storey in his lifetime was the address before the New England Suffrage Conference, which took place on March 30, 1903. While speaking on the title, *Negro Suffrage is not a Failure*, he began by reminding his audience that the Fifteenth Amendment had become a part of the Constitution thirty years before the speech. This meant that the citizenship and rights of African Americans to liberty, property, and life had already been guaranteed by the Fourteenth Amendment, which also protected them from any denial of their voting rights because of race.[76]

The long struggle for justice for African Americans came to an end with the adoption of the amendment. According to Storey, those who established a new nation conceived in liberty and dedication to the belief that all men are created equal were unable to execute what they believed in, and he summarized their actions with the words of Emerson:

> *"They overlooked the moral law and winked at a practical exception to the bill of rights they had drawn up. They winked at the exception, believing it insignificant. But the moral law, the nature of things, did not wink at it, but kept its eyes wide open. It turned out that this one violation was a subtle poison, which in eighty years corrupted the whole body politic, and brought the alternative of extirpation of the poison or ruin to the republic."*

Even when they insisted that all men were created with an equal right to life and liberty, they still enslaved about half a million men while feeling that their attempts to continue depriving them of their rights were safe. Unfortunately, irrepressible conflict followed, further increasing the rate of violence and bitterness and eventually leading to the Civil War, accompanied by so much suffering and loss.

Storey was firmly convinced that the suffering and loss of the war was the penalty that the nation had to pay for embracing a policy of injustice. In his view, it was only after much suffering that the people finally agreed to do what was right. So, amid the wounds and hurts of the war, men who supported the enslavement and deprivation of the rights of Blacks finally agreed to do justice and ensure equal rights for all men, and this was added to the fundamental laws.

In his speech, he described the event as a momentous one and remarked that it was at that point that the nation attained its highest moral level. It was the moment when the people shared the same faith with Charles Sumner when he declared:

"Show me a creature with lifted countenance looking to heaven, made in the image of God, and I show you a Man who of whatever country or race, whether bronzed by equatorial sun or blanched by polar cold, is with you a child of the Heavenly Father, and equal with you in all the fights of human nature."

He observed that the course where equal rights were secured for all men – African Americans and whites – was not questioned, especially in the North. This seemed to suggest that it was challenged in the South. It is interesting to note that Storey described individuals who guarded the equal rights of all men and voting rights for Blacks as prophets and saints. Among those listed as examples were Lincoln, Chase, Seward, Andrew, and, of course, the list would not have been complete without Charles Sumner.

In Storey's view, the progress that had been made after several decades of struggle was now being threatened by a group of people claimed that treating Blacks as citizens and their right to vote was a mistake, and that they should be deprived of the voting rights that, in Storey's view, were only being enjoyed in theory. He cited the statements of several politicians who spoke against voting rights for Blacks and among them were Dr. Lyman Abbott and Secretary Root.[76]

Undoubtedly, Storey did not support those who claimed that Black suffrage was a failure. He was firmly against the numerous attacks on the voting rights of African Americans and took his time to provide a brief history of how the nation granted Blacks the right to vote. His address was a wake-up call for people to uphold the rights of African Americans.

REFERENCES

1. Bio Moorfield. Massachusetts Historical Society; 1931.

2. Allen, J. W. Moorfield Storey: 1845-1929, *American Bar Association Journal.* Massachusetts Historical Society.

3. Coles, E., & Sullivan, J. Moorfield Storey Papers. A Finding Aid to the Collection in the Library of Congress; 2010.

4. Austrian, G. Moorfield Storey, Brief life of a patrician reformer: 1845-1929; 2018.

5. Teresa, S. M. Family Recollections, 1925.

6. Peron, J. Moorfield Storey: The Unknown Libertarian, 2018.

7. Daugherity, B. Moorfield Storey (1845-1929), Civil liberties in the United States; 2012.

8. Committee on the Negro "Call" for a National Conference, February 1909. [Internet]. Typescript. Page 2 - Page 3 Ray Stannard Baker Papers, Manuscript Division, Library of Congress (018.00.00) Digital ID # na0018p1. Available from: http://www. loc.gov/exhibits/naacp/founding-and-early-years.html#obj2

9. Harvard University, Class of 1866. (1866-1931). Secretary's Report.

10. Wikipedia. (n.d). Charles Sumner.

11. Moorfield, S. Charles Sumner. Boston, New York: Houghton, Mifflin and Company; 1900.

12. Perry, B. Moorfield Storey as a Man. The Crisis, Page 157-57; 1930.

13. Howe, De Wolf. M. A. Moorfield Storey, Pattern of The Intellectual Rebel, The New York Times; 1932.

14. Storey, M. Obedience to the Law: An Address at the Opening of Petigru College in Columbia, South Carolina.

15. Storey, M. GOVERNMENT CONTROL; The Words of an Eminent Men on the "Passion for Regulative Legislation;" 1919.

16. Storey, M. The Independent Man. The New York Times; 1891.

17. Storey, M. Moorfield Storey of Boston Bar Denounces His Action in New England Railroad Litigation, CALLS CLIENT A DUMMY. New York Times; 1916.

18. Storey, M. Time to Check Corruption; 1894.

19. Beisner, Robert L. Twelve against Empire: The Anti-Imperialists, 1898–1900. New York: McGraw-Hill; 1968.

20. Welch, Richard E., Jr. The Presidencies of Grover Cleveland. Lawrence: University Press of Kansas; 1988.

21. Wiebe, Robert H. Self-Rule: A Cultural History of American Democracy. Chicago: University of Chicago Press; 1995.

22. Jensen, Richard. The Winning of the Midwest: Social and Political Conflict, 1888–1896. Chicago: University of Chicago Press; 1971.

23. Kleppner, Paul. The Third Electoral System: Parties, Voters, and Political Cultures, 1853–1892. Chapel Hill: University of North Carolina Press; 1979.

24. Jones, Stanley L. The Presidential Election of 1896. Madison: University of Wisconsin Press; 1964.

25. Ritter, Gretchen. Goldbugs and Greenbacks: The Antimonopoly Tradition and the Politics of Finance in America. New York: Cambridge University Press; 1997.

26. Higgs, Robert. Crisis and Leviathan: Critical Episodes in the Growth of American Government; 1987.

27. Timberlake, Richard H. Monetary Policy in the United States: An Intellectual and Institutional History. Chicago: University of Chicago Press; [1978] 1993.

28. Tucker, David M. Mugwumps: Public Moralists of the Gilded Age. Columbia: University of Missouri Press; 1998.

29. McFarland, Gerald W. The Mugwumps and the Emergence of Modern America. In Moralists or Pragmatists? The Mugwumps, 1884–1900, edited by Gerald McFarland. New York: Simon and Schuster; 1975.

30. Williamson, Harold Francis. Edward Atkinson: The Biography of an American Liberal, 1827–1905. Boston: Old Corner Book Store; 1934.

31. Logsdon, Joseph. Horace White, Nineteenth-Century Liberal. Westport, Conn.: Greenwood Publishing; 1971.

32. Fleming, E. McClung. R. R. Bowker: Militant Liberal. Norman: University of Oklahoma Press; 1952.

33. Hixson, William B., Jr. Moorfield Storey and the Abolitionist Tradition. New York: Oxford University Press. New York: Oxford University Press; 1972.

34. Beito, D., & Beito, L. R. Gold Democrats and the Decline of Classical Liberalism, 1896–1900.

35. Storey, M. Nothing to Excuse Our Intervention: President's Speech at the Meeting of the Massachusetts Reform Club; April 8, 1898.

36. Storey, M. Charles Sumner: Mr. Moorfield Storey's Biography of the Great Senator. New York Times; 1900.

37. Social Circle in Concord. (May 25, 1903). The Centenary of the birth of Ralph Waldo Emerson: as observed in Concord.

38. Moorfield Storey to George L. Fox, 2 February 1904, Moorfield Storey papers, Massachusetts Historical Society.

39. Moorfield Storey to Charles E. Ward, 30 March 1906, Moorfield Storey papers, Massachusetts Historical Society.

40. Moorfield Storey to Francis B. Sears, 6 May 1911, Moorfield Storey papers, Massachusetts Historical Society.

41. Moorfield Storey to George H. St. Tucker, 6 May 1912, Moorfield Storey papers, Massachusetts Historical Society.

42. Moorfield Storey to Prof. Dr. Theodore Schott, 19 December 1912, Moorfield Storey papers, Massachusetts Historical Society.

43. Moorfield Storey to Col. N. P. Hallowell, 22 April 1912, Moorfield Storey papers, Massachusetts Historical Society.

44. Moorfield Storey to William M. Trotter, 30 December 1910, Moorfield Storey papers, Massachusetts Historical Society.

45. Moorfield Storey to George H. St. Tucker, 6 May 1912, Moorfield Storey papers, Massachusetts Historical Society.

46. Du Bois, W.E.B. *The Negro's Fatherland.* Massachusetts Historical Society; 1917.

47. Finkelman, P. The Encyclopedia of American Civil Liberties: A - F, Index. ISBN 9780415943420, Published by Routledge 2304 Pages; 2007.

48. Guinn v. United States - Civil Rights and Wrongs - Court, Decision, NAACP, and Law - JRank Articles [Internet]. Available from: https://law.jrank.org/pages/24877/Guinn-v-United-States-Civil-Rights-Wrongs.html#ixzz6t7v8ua3y

49. Longley, R. Guinn v. United States: A First Step to Voter Rights for Black Americans, ThoughtCo. [Internet]. 2020.

50. Herbin-Triant, E. The forgotten civil rights case that stopped the spread of Jim Crow. Washington Post [Internet]. 2017. Available from: https://www.washingtonpost.com/news/made-by-history/wp/2017/11/05/

the-forgotten-civil-rights-case-that-stopped-the-spread-of-jim-crow/

51. Finkelman, P. Buchanan v. Warley, 245 U.S. 60 (1917), Civil Liberties and Civil Rights in the United States [Internet]. 2012. Available from: https://U.S.civilliberties.org/cases/3257-buchanan-v-warley-245-U.S.-60-1917.html

52. Miller, E. The Neglected Case of Buchanan v. Warly, Scotus. Blog; 2010.

53. Buchanan v. Warley - Significance - Rights, Decision, Ordinance, and Justice - JRank Articles [Internet]. Available from: https://law.jrank.org/pages/24788/Buchanan-v-Warley-Significance.html#ixzz6t905VCDy

54. Uenuma, F. The Massacre of Black Sharecroppers That Led the Supreme Court to Curb the Racial Disparities of the Justice System, Smithsonian Magazine; 2018.

55. New York Times. Negroes Beg Lives of Supreme Court; 1923.

56. Wikipedia. (n.d). Elaine Massacre.

57. Moorfield, S. Letter from Moorfield Storey to Walter F. White. [Internet]. Digital Commonwealth Massachusetts Collections Online; 1925. Available from: https://www.digitalcommonwealth.org/search/commonwealth-oai:9s16bx382

58. White, W. F. Massacring Whites" in Arkansas, The Nation. [Internet]. 1919. Available from: https://www.unz.com/print/Nation-1919dec06-00714?__cf_chl_jschl_tk__=f9cdafe-fe3e44ba32f193bfa30b2f61ce6ee7426-1593063875-0-AYM_4FTYfDZ4KTvjQiyfHxcRW8GZXAtAQMTBru_UH0BlYbYs2oJZa5I9ksgZCgIU36VLJ-VMNhG9Yhw7t7dEcSybUx0_WXOW3Y5eQMy6yhRXQbe2yqr3bghyiKPinGpRDsR0wQ-Jpas3W1Vs2P0RljUmkBvQHbOklcOgARA3QFzANG5rjbht_VU677laacTYa3YNMFrtqZOo-_Pxo-GG_KsdwtntDn8PB-gWHsPkf52UjonUgd2ITz6dlWOdRwIZlrgzczrPQSbylZYwwN6sqjw1ju-WSZGM9fVd7aohRoxQ3DpxZRFBbICDoE-5JKY1SB9GA

59. Wikipedia: the free encyclopedia [Internet]. Walter Francis White. [Updated 13 October 2021; cited 2021 November 20]; https://en.wikipedia.org/wiki/Walter_Francis_White

60. JRank Articles. Voting Rights - Discriminatory Practices - Primary, White, Court, and Nixon.

61. The Crisis. From Grandfather Clause to Voting Rights Act. NAACP in vanguard of fight for the Ballot; 1984. Vol. 91 No. 8 (386).

62. Storey, M. The Negro Question, An Address Delivered Before the Wisconsin Bar Association. Reprinted by the National Association for the Advancement of Colored People; 1918. [Internet]. Available from: https://archive.org/details/negro-qestwiscbar00storrich/page/n3/mode/2up?q=Moorfield+Sto-rey%E2%80%99s+Address+to+Wisconsin+Bar+Association

63. New York Times. To Make Strikes Crimes: That is the Proposition Moorfield Storey Urges before Bar Association; 1919.

64. Storey, M. THE LEAGUE AS SAFEGUARD; TrU.S.t in Our Allies is Needed if We Would Keep the Fruits of Victory. New York Times; 1919.

65. New York Times. For Anti-Lynching Bill: Moorfield Storey Makes Plea in Newark for Passage of Measure. New York Times; 1922.

66. New York Times. Make Final Pleas on Industrial Court: Moorfield Storey Appears for Kansas in Howat Suit Before Supreme Court; 1922.

67. NAACP. Seventeenth Annual Convention, *Massachusetts Historical Society.* The Chicago Evening Post, Chicago, Ill; 1926.

68. Hope, J. Southern College President Sees Era of Improved Race Relations, *Massachusetts Historical Society*; 1926.

69. The NAACP. *Its History Achievements Purposes.* Massachusetts Historical Society.

70. The New York Times On October 24, 1929, The New York Times announced the passing away of Moorfield Storey; 1929.

71. Eskridge, W. N. Some Effects of Identity-Based Social Movements on Constitutional Law in the Twentieth Century, Yale Law School [Internet]. 2002. Vol. 100, Iss. 8, 2062-2407 Available from: https://digitalcommons.law.yale.edu/cgi/viewcontent.cgi?article=4785&context=fss_papers

72. Finkelman, P. The Encyclopedia of American Civil Liberties: A - F, Index; 2006. ISBN 9780415943420, Published by Routledge 2304 Pages.

73. Finkelman, P. Buchanan v. Warley, 245 U.S. 60 (1917), Civil Liberties and Civil Rights in the United States. [Internet]. 2012. Available from: https://U.S.civilliberties.org/cases/3257-buchanan-v-warley-245-U.S.-60-1917.html

74. Gougeon, L. Virtue's Hero: Emerson, Anti-slavery, and Reform. Page 344-348; 1990.

75. Mudge, J. M. Emerson's Revolution: Page 257-258; 2015.

76. Storey, M. Negro Suffrage is not a Failure: An address before the New England Suffrage Conference, March 30, 1903. [Internet]. Library of Congress, Boston: Geo. H. Ellis Co., Printers. Available from: https://www.loc.gov/resource/rbaapc.27900/?sp=6&st=text

ABOUT THE AUTHOR

Elvis Slaughter, MSCJ, enjoys writing works of fiction and nonfiction based on his extensive criminology experience. He is the author of several published articles and eleven books. Elvis is a lifetime member of the NAACP, educator, and community activist.

OTHER BOOKS BY ELVIS SLAUGHTER

1. 978-0-9791461-1-4 Uncle Percy's Blessings, Hardback, 5 ¾ x 8 ¾, 2005

2. 978-0-9791461-9-0 Malcolm X Project, Paperback, 5 ½ x 8 ½, 2010

3. 978-0-9791461-5-2 The American Genocide, Paperback, 6 x 9, 2008

4. 978-1-4196622-9-4 Ghosts of Hollandale, Paperback, 6 x 9, 2006

5. 978-0-9965932-4-3 Egomaniac, Paperback, 6 x 9, 2015

6. 978-0-9965932-8-1 Preschool To Prison, Paperback, 6 x 9, 2017

7. 978-0-9965932-5-0 Safer Jail and Prison Matters, Paperback, 6 x 9, 2016

8. 978-0-9965932-7-4 Egomaniac, Ebook, 2016

9. 978-0-9965932-6-7 Safer Jail and Prison Matters, Ebook, 2016

10. 978-0-9965932-3-6 Malcolm X Project, Ebook, 2010

11. 978-0-9965932-2-9 Epiphany Or Sin, Ebook, 2015

12. 978-0-9965932-1-2 Epiphany Or Sin, Hardback, 2015, 6 x 9

13. 978-0-9965932-0-5 Epiphany Or Sin Paperback-Cancelled, 6 x 9, 2015

14. 978-0-9791461-0-7 Uncle Percy's Blessings, Paperback, 8.5 x 8.5, 2006

15. 978-0-9965932-7-4 Egomaniac, Ebook, 2016

16. 878-0-9791461-5-2 The American Genocide, Ebook, 2008

17. 978-0-9791461-4-5 The Malcolm X Project, Ebook, 2010

18. 978-0-9965932-3-6 The Malcolm X Project, Ebook, 2010

19. 978-0-9791461-2-1 Uncle Percy's Blessings, Paperback, 2007

20. 978-1-7360506-2-0 Mentally ILL Inmate and Corrections, Paperback, 6 x 9, 2021

21. 978-1-7360506-0-6 Spector, Paperback, 2020

CPSIA information can be obtained
at www.ICGtesting.com
Printed in the USA
LVHW110755030722
722658LV00002B/3